Praise for *Move the Room*

"This book will transform the way you deliver a speech, close a deal, or motivate your team. Even the most seasoned and effective public speakers will find something new and useful in Trevor Currie's insightful book."

DANIEL H. PINK #1 *New York Times*-bestselling author of *When*, *Drive*, and *To Sell Is Human*

"*Move the Room* is an extraordinarily practical book for speakers who want to persuade or motivate in settings large or small. It is based on acute observation of both speakers and audiences that has been translated into practical advice that anyone can use."

NIGEL WRIGHT senior managing director, Onex Corporation; former chief of staff to the prime minister of Canada

"I've watched Trevor Currie turn the most timid speakers into extraordinary presenters. This book breaks down the how-to, but not with a series of gimmicks or tricks. It is a systemic analysis of great presenters and presentations—an incredible gift to all who aspire to master speaking to groups of people large and small."

JON LAX vice president, product design, Facebook Reality Labs

"*Move the Room* combines practical insights and real-life examples to illustrate how speaking opportunities can become force multipliers that propel you to accomplish more. Trevor Currie blends wit and wisdom to show how effective speaking is at the center of so many leaders' success."

DUNCAN L. SINCLAIR chair, Deloitte LLP Canada and Chile

"Trevor Currie captures lightning in a bottle with his latest book, *Move the Room*, which delivers smart, practical approaches and insights essential for delivering powerful and unforgettable keynotes, confidently closing a deal, or simply inspiring your team."

DOUG MURPHY CEO, Corus Entertainment Inc.

"Drawing on years of presentation consulting and in-depth analysis of many of the world's most famous speakers, Trevor Currie teaches even the most unsure speakers how to own the stage. A must-read for aspiring and seasoned professionals."

CAMERON FOWLER chief strategy and operations officer, BMO Financial Group

"*Move the Room* is a must-read guide for effective communications, demystifying the art of storytelling with inspiring, real-life examples. For anyone who aspires to generate buy-in with a newfound sense of confidence and impact, Trevor Currie's book will forever change your audiences' perceptions of you and your ideas."

MIYO YAMASHITA president and CEO, The Princess Margaret Cancer Foundation

"*Move the Room* is jam-packed with actionable advice and animated with instructive and inspiring examples. An easy and worthwhile read, this book offers practical tools for improving your speaking and enhancing your profile in the market."

STEPHANIE WILLSON chief client relations and marketing officer, Blake, Cassels & Graydon LLP

"If I take away just one valuable tip from a business book, it will have been time well spent. As I read *Move the Room*, I found myself repeatedly saying, 'That's so good!' Unlike other business books, you'll want to keep reading because the strategies are quick, and written in Trevor Currie's friendly, witty way. This book will build your skills and confidence as you learn to improve your craft of speaking and leading."

ALISON LEUNG head of marketing, Canada, Shopify

"Two parts pragmatic advice, one part inspiration, *Move the Room* will help you stand apart in a professional crowd by mastering public speaking. Trevor Currie's career of coaching high-performance speakers is evident throughout, and this book will become a go-to guide for the occasional presenter all the way to the seasoned orator."

DAVID MORGENSTERN senior managing director, Accenture

"I have seen first-hand the transformation of those who have worked with Trevor Currie. They have all successfully taken their speaking skills to the next level by learning how to effectively deliver their message with confidence, clarity, and persuasiveness. Through this book, leaders and influencers everywhere can now access Trevor's brilliant insights and practical approach. It's a career game changer!"

DEBORAH M. DALFEN chief professional resources officer, Torys LLP

"*Move the Room* is chock-full of real-life stories and actionable takeaways for anyone who needs to move their audience to take action. If you're in the business of influencing others, *Move the Room* gives you an unfair advantage."

JOHN WARRILLOW founder, The Value Builder System; author of *Built to Sell*, *The Automatic Customer*, and *The Art of Selling Your Business*

"The deep insights and reliable strategies in *Move the Room* turns the fear of public speaking on its head. It allows you to address the subjects that may make us feel most vulnerable, which deep within we understand is the key to connecting to others on a truly authentic and inspirational level."

JEFF DAVIS chief legal and corporate affairs officer, Ontario Teachers' Pension Plan

"This book gives you the keys to kingdom: The 'how' of effective communication, illustrated powerfully and practically."

BRUCE SELLERY bestselling author of *Moolala*; money columnist, CBC

SEVEN SECRETS OF EXTRAORDINARY SPEAKERS

TREVOR CURRIE

MOVE THE ROOM

PAGE TWO

Some names and identifying details have been
changed to protect the privacy of individuals.

Cataloguing in publication information is available
from Library and Archives Canada.
ISBN 978-1-77458-137-7 (paperback)
ISBN 978-1-77458-138-4 (ebook)

Page Two
pagetwo.com

Edited by Scott Steedman
Copyedited by Jenny Govier
Proofread by Alison Strobel
Cover design by Peter Cocking
Interior design and illustrations by Fiona Lee

movetheroom.ca

To Clara, Evan, and Rae-Lee

CONTENTS

INTRODUCTION:
SPEAKING IS A FORCE MULTIPLIER 1

Changing Perceptions in Twenty
Minutes after Twenty Years 5

The Expert's Paradox 6

1 SHRINK THE WALL 9

Pink's Surprising Truth 11

The Strategic Flip 13

The Second Filter Set 21

2 CREATE AN IDEA QUIVER 25

Commanding Opening 26

Statement of Purpose 28

Essential Messages 29

Power Messages to Build
Support and Proof 33

Connect the Compartments 34

Pulling It Together 34

Closing with Power 35

3 ADD POWER MESSAGES 39

Balcony Heroes 39

Examples 44

Storytelling 49

Analogy and Metaphor 78

Quotations 88

Testimony 92

Data 96

The Communication Trifecta 102

4 USE ENABLING VISUALS 107

Differentiating in the Desert 108

The Waste of Cut and Paste 110

An Image to Rattle and Rally 112

Enforcing the Code 114

The Multi-Million-Dollar Marker 115

Synthetic What? 116

Anchor a Theme 117

Branding Bankruptcy 118

Show the Spread 120

Cutts's Rut-Breaking Recipe 121

Bad Math and Bad Slides 121

Beware the Millstone of Handouts 122

Don't Compete with Your Slides 125

5 CLOSE THE CIRCUIT 127

Mr. Reckless Abandon
Wrecked Himself 127

Eye Contact 128

Don't Confuse Awkwardness
with Ineffectiveness 134

Conversational Tone 135

Animating Your Hands and Voice 136

Composure, Hands Edition 142

Framing, Light, and
Sound for Video Talks 144

Pace and Pause 145

Charisma Killers—Disfluencies
and Filler 154

Uncertainty and Upspeak 155

Reference Back 156

Interaction 157

Add Levity 158

Anchor Your Feet 164

6 CAPITALIZE ON QUESTIONS 167

Four Letters Cratered a Campaign 167

To Respond or Not to Respond 169

Risk Management Meets Tough Questions 170

Q&A Composure 171

Uh-Oh, I Don't Know 172

Disarming and Defusing Sticky Situations 174

Tactics to Be Used in Moderation 175

7 COMPOUND YOUR CONFIDENCE 177

A Nervous Anchor 177

Return on Rehearsal 178

Transparency Is an Illusion 181

The Bootcamp Boost 181

Focus Outwardly 183

The Pursuit of Peace 184

Confidence for Sunday 185

Confidence Begets Confidence 186

CONCLUSION: MOVING MILLIONS 189

ACKNOWLEDGMENTS 191

NOTES 193

RESOURCES: NOTEWORTHY TALKS 200

INTRODUCTION
SPEAKING IS A
FORCE MULTIPLIER

"**I**'M AFRAID IF I call you a researcher, no one will come because they'll think you're boring and irrelevant," an event planner said to Dr. Brown after inviting her to speak at a conference. Ouch. None of us wants to be boring and irrelevant. But Brown was not a known speaker, and the event planner was struggling with how to describe her in a way that would build interest for her talk.

"The thing I like about your talk is you're a storyteller. So I think what I'll do is just call you a storyteller," said the planner. The professor quickly admitted she felt insecure being described as a storyteller. She's a researcher. After some reflection, she came up with a compromise. "I'm a qualitative researcher. I collect stories; that's what I do. Why don't you just say I'm a researcher-storyteller."[1]

"Ha-ha. There's no such thing," said the planner, denying the idea.

Brown might not have won in the chat about how to describe herself, but to say she won over a Houston audience she went

1

on to recount this story to is a gross understatement. Wearing a loose-fitting brown blouse, black jeans, and gold hoop earrings, she moved the room with her research storytelling.

Some of the stories were personal. She admitted to having a breakdown that prompted her to ask her friends for therapist recommendations. "Whoa, I wouldn't want to be *your* therapist," they said. This pairing of humility and humor is threaded through her talks. She draws you in and disarms you, giving you a chance to see yourself and others a little bit differently.

"I told these 500 people that I had a breakdown. I had a slide that said 'Breakdown.' At what point did I think that was a good idea?" she said to a friend a few days after that Houston talk. "YouTube, they're putting this thing on YouTube. And we're going to be talking about 600, 700 people." The prospect of this happening had her joke that she would break in and steal the video footage and destroy it before it could be posted.[2]

That Houston talk was a critical inflection point in her career, but not in the way she feared. Within a decade the video had been watched over 60 million times.[3] Brené Brown went from doing research at the third-largest university in Houston to writing five #1 *New York Times*-bestselling books.[4] She has been Oprah's guest on *Super Soul Sunday*. She now has a six-figure speaking fee and delivers twenty-five to fifty talks per year. Brown provides leadership advice to companies like Pixar, IBM, and the Seattle Seahawks and has influenced millions, including Melinda Gates and Hollywood moguls.[5] Netflix filmed her lecture "The Call to Courage" and shared it with the world in April 2019, a first for any researcher. She was a featured guest on *60 Minutes* at the start of the global pandemic in 2020, soothing a scared nation. That's a lot of impact for a researcher.

Was the quality of Brown's research better the month after she gave her TED talk than the month before it? No. But many more people recognized and valued her work after her talk. This shift in profile after a talk is not unique to Brown. The magnitude of the shift may have been, but the underlying phenomenon wasn't.

Speaking is a force multiplier. If you are better at speaking, people will value you and your capabilities more. You will be more in demand. Combine the skill of speaking with any other skill and you will multiply your impact in that area and beyond.

The term "force multiplier" is rooted in the military. It refers to a factor that allows you to accomplish greater feats than you could without it. Night vision goggles are a force multiplier. They allow an army to have, say, a tenfold impact over a similar army without night vision.

Speaking is a force multiplier for Brown, and her experience is not an aberration. A two-year freshman senator spoke at a convention in Boston in 2004. Few outside the state of Illinois had heard of him before the talk. Afterward, tens of millions had. Speaking is a force multiplier for Barack Obama. It helped him ascend from being a community organizer to holding the most powerful seat in the world. Time and again, we've seen outlier speakers make an outsize impact. What's different about them?

Both Brown and Obama have compelling content and are in the room when they speak: they make it seem like they are talking directly to you, and they move you. It's rare. It's valuable. And it's powerful.

If you want to move the room—galvanize a team, stir souls, spark insights—you need strong content, and you must be in the room when you deliver it. Powerful speaking will lift your leadership and help you put your dent in the universe. This book will teach you how.

**A successful talk is a little miracle—
people see the world differently afterward.**

CHRIS ANDERSON, TED CURATOR

There are loads of mediocre speakers out there and precious few great ones. It doesn't take a lot to separate yourself from the masses and shine. You just need to do a few things a little bit differently and better. In the coming pages, I will give you a playbook so you can speak effectively to any audience: a process to prepare, frame, and deliver engaging and compelling communication. This process will increase the consistency of your success and confidence as a speaker.

The concepts and approaches will be brought to life with instructive and inspiring examples of extraordinary speakers from the TED stage to the C-suite. TED speakers tend to be subject matter experts who are talking about their expertise to an intelligent audience that doesn't share their technical background. In other words, they're very similar to most of my clients—and likely similar to you.

People love TED talks and share them widely. To help understand why, I've analyzed the top 100 TED talks (the "Top 100") across more than fifty measures in three categories: content, delivery, and slides. These talks were selected by their combined view counts on TED.com and YouTube and have been watched online over 1 billion times. In the Resources, I've listed the top talks I refer to throughout this book. In the following seven chapters, I will reveal their secrets and the unconventional approaches stemming from this analysis of what makes speakers extraordinary. I will share data from the analysis to help you to make better choices. The data is meant to be provocative, not prescriptive. In the event there's a gap between your current practice and the best approaches, you'll have good ideas about how to close it and move the room.

In this book I will also integrate examples from my practice of twenty-four years helping leaders to prep for high-stakes talks to help you improve yours. These techniques will be bolstered with academic research to give you confidence to grow in research-grounded ways.

The rewards for improving are real and readily achievable. One of my clients, who leads a global professional service firm, remarked on how becoming a better speaker changed how others see him.

Changing Perceptions in Twenty Minutes after Twenty Years

"I've seen you speak for twenty years and I've never seen you speak like that. The hair on the back of my neck stood up—and it doesn't move for much. I'm a tough marker and you scored big." This is what Mateo heard after stepping off the stage at the Fairmont Vancouver during a global gathering of the professional services firm he was leading.

Mateo is the kind of leader who compels people to declare how much they love him. He listens to you with the rare, rapt attention we all crave but never seem to get. He remembers what you told him in the past, from the professional (why the firm should pursue a market segment) to the personal (the name of your spouse and what instrument you played decades prior). He would be the last to reference his advanced degree from Harvard, but the first to make fun of his many foibles: "You couldn't even count on me to carry the basketball onto the court, much less shoot it."

The love for Mateo is well deserved. Yet until Vancouver, he wasn't loved as a speaker. Since then, if you ask a dozen people from his firm to name an impressive and inspiring speaker from the industry, as I have done over the years, his name comes up most often. He moves people, and his enhanced speaking has changed how others see him as a leader. As he told me, "I have been transformed and empowered through becoming a better speaker."

Mateo went on to say this:

> There is a halo effect that comes from performing effectively in front of groups of people—because the ability to do that is relatively scarce, I find that people generalize from that ability and make all kinds of assumptions about the ability of the person to do *other*, unrelated things competently. So, because I can pull off a presentation in front of a large group without falling completely on my face, they actually think I can carry off other aspects of my job in similar fashion. They wouldn't come to that conclusion based on a strong analytical piece that I write (if I could!). While this merely delays the day when it will be discovered that the emperor has no clothes, it is quite handy in the meantime.

You will spend years—decades—building up your expertise. You can transform your self-perception and how others see you in minutes when you move the room.

The Expert's Paradox

So many speakers' efforts are thwarted by the very thing they've worked so hard at building, and the very thing that brought them up onto the stage: expertise.

"Whereas I would've considered using your firm in the past, now you're off the list," Nancy told me one participant wrote on the feedback form after a colleague's presentation in the late nineties. Others didn't get the chance to write feedback because they walked out before the talk was over. What went wrong?

The disastrous end had a simple beginning. "I've worked for years to build my expertise. I want to raise my profile in the market to build more demand for our services. Can you help me put on a speaking event?" Nancy, the head of marketing at a major national consultancy, gets requests like this weekly from partners who want to raise their profile. She and her team booked a downtown ballroom, filled it with high-value prospective clients—managers of big businesses looking for practical solutions to their knottiest problems. The firm's banners were hung high above the platform, catering was ordered, an AV company was hired, and the stage was ready. All the expert had to do was show up and speak well.

But he fell victim to the Expert's Paradox.

People attended the event because they wanted to learn from the expert. Paradoxically, the biggest impediment to him connecting with them was his expertise: He covered way too much technical content, which he had put on way too many slides. And then he got up and read bullet. After bullet. After bullet.

The talk was chock-full of technical, abstract theory, and forty-five minutes of dry detail delivered in a monotone. He read foundational definitions—things you would expect him to rattle off while operating a backhoe. He even read his name in a way that made it seem like he had no idea who he was.

"We will never host another event again unless the speaker commits to getting coaching. Otherwise, it's just not worth our firm's resources and reputation," Nancy told me when she called to commiserate—and create a better approach. So began my business, with Nancy as my first major client. I've been working with the firm every year since.

The Expert's Paradox is pervasive. "Thinking through all the possibilities makes you a great practitioner. But speaking to all the possibilities will make you a bad speaker," said Markus Koehnen, who practiced complex commercial litigation for twenty-nine years before being appointed to the Superior Court of Justice in Ontario. It's easy for experts to suffer from this paradox. This is true whether you are in tech, tax, management consulting, law, advertising, or finance.

How do jurors assess the credibility of an expert witness? Research shows the most important factor is not the number of degrees or the institution where they were earned. Nor is it the wearing of studious-looking spectacles. It is clarity. If you are an expert, you are expected to be able to explain things clearly.[6] People work for decades to build expertise through school, apprenticeships, and on-the-job training. But most spend mere minutes learning how to communicate about their expertise clearly.

The next step will be time well spent. It will take you from being an expert to being seen as one. It will set you up to multiply your force and move the room.

1

SHRINK THE WALL

"I WAS ABOUT TO finish my first year at university and I was worried about my mounting student debt. What job would you do if you wanted to make as much money as you could with the few skills that you had?" Ryan asked me.

"I don't know—construction?" I guessed.

"Sales. I got a job in retail. That's where I learned the importance of shrinking the wall."

Ryan is driven, outgoing, and competitive. He landed a commission-based sales position at a footwear retailer. The kind of place that makes the sales staff dress in synthetic referee jerseys. "I remember saying to my girlfriend, Katie, 'I'm going to be the top salesperson,' before I started. How much did I sell in the first week? Next to nothing. I was humbled. But I was determined, so I asked the most seasoned sales rep for some help," he said.

Ryan told me that he had misread the sales rep and her sales capabilities. Unlike him, she had neither the physique of an athlete nor the charisma of a class president. But she was smart. And fortunately for Ryan, she was generous with her advice. "You're trying to sell the whole wall of shoes. That's a shortcut to an empty paycheck," she told him.

"Yeah, the path to poverty is not what I'm after—please tell me more," he replied.

"I've watched you on the floor. You have a quick conversation with the customer before heading into the stockroom and coming out with a tower of boxes of shoes."

He shook his head. "I know. It seems like they spend the next half hour trying on all the products, buying none, and I spend the next fifteen minutes stuffing tissue back in shoes and restocking the storeroom. I've got to admit, I thought you were lazy," he said, commenting that he noticed she didn't bring many pairs out.

"Never more than three," she said.

"How do you know which three to get?"

"That's where you ask the key questions to help you shrink the wall: How do you plan to use the shoes? Do you have any brand preferences? What is your budget?" She gave Ryan a moment to absorb before she continued. "Once you know the answers to these questions, you can confidently pick the right shoes for them."

She explained that knowing the right shoes to present is half the challenge. The other half is using the Power Messages that we will address later in this book.

Ryan is a quick study. Before long he was the number one salesperson, a position he maintained for the balance of the summer. His customers bought one pair 70 percent of the time, and 5 percent of the time they bought two—far better than his first week of trying to sell the whole wall.

This isn't about selling shoes. It's about strategically picking the right ideas to put forward based on what's important to your listener. After graduating from university, Ryan joined an agency that had $5 million in annual revenue. Five years later they had grown to $300 million. Guess who their top business developer was. Years later Ryan became a professional fund-raiser for a leading cancer research hospital, where he quickly became a top fundraiser. Shrinking the Wall applies to all domains, from politics to pediatrics to intellectual property.

Oral communication is an inefficient medium to be comprehensive. Too many professionals try to sell the whole wall of shoes, whether they are on stage, in a boardroom, or on a video call. It's a losing game. There are other ways better suited for getting a lot of info out, such as a book, a white paper, or a memo. But not a speaking engagement. The last thing your audience wants is to listen to someone read a treatise to them in a monotone. Don't be the bore in the ballroom.

> **The secret to being a bore is telling everything.**
> VOLTAIRE

Speaking *is* a great way to focus your audience's attention on the most important ideas that are relevant to their pressing needs. If you treat speaking as a sampling exercise where you will give your listeners a small taste of a much bigger offering, they will have an appetite for more of your ideas and capabilities.

Pink's Surprising Truth

Dan Pink is a master shrink—he knows how to Shrink the Wall, that is, and build demand.

How do you motivate creative problem-solving? It's an important question, and Pink has the answer. As the developed world has advanced from the industrial to the information age, professionals have put an increased emphasis on right-brained, creative problem-solving. If we can get more people to be better at it, we can move toward a more prosperous and sustainable future.

Dan Pink spent years studying motivation. He wrote up his findings in his bestselling book, *Drive: The Surprising Truth about What Motivates Us*. In it he summarizes our three central motivators: autonomy, mastery, and purpose. "There is a mismatch between what science knows and what business does," Pink said in "The Puzzle of Motivation," the 2009 TED talk based on his book.

Did he get up on stage and read from it? No, he's a former chief speechwriter for Vice President Al Gore, and he knows better. Did he talk about all three themes in his talk? No, he talked about one: autonomy.

He illustrated it with inspiring examples. He explained that great ideas are spawned when people are given the freedom to choose what problems to work on. Engineers at Google can spend 20 percent of their time working on whatever they want. This autonomy includes creating their own team, time, and approach to tackling their challenge. About half of all new products at Google can trace their origins to 20 percent autonomous time, including Gmail and Google News.

Pink added more examples to show that when you give people the opportunity to self-direct, their productivity, worker engagement, and satisfaction all go up and turnover goes down.

"Some of you may look at this and say, 'Hmm, that sounds nice, but it's utopian,'" Pink said, revealing his knack for anticipating what the audience is thinking and lining up his next point to address it. In his roomy jeans and mauve dress shirt, he animated his messages with gestures that separated what science knows and what business does. "In the mid-1990s,

Microsoft started an encyclopedia called Encarta. They had deployed all the right incentives. They paid professionals to write and edit thousands of articles. Well-compensated managers oversaw the whole thing to make sure it came in on budget and on time."

He contrasted that approach with another that got started a few years later, where no one gets paid, they just work on the encyclopedia for fun: Wikipedia.

To close out his argument in favor of intrinsic, self-directed motivators, Pink spoke to those in the audience with a left-brained bias. "Just ten years ago, if you had gone to an economist, anywhere, and said, 'Hey, I got these two different models for creating an encyclopedia—if they went head-to-head, who would win?' Ten years ago you would not have found a single sober economist anywhere on planet Earth who would have predicted the Wikipedia model."

Wikipedia is one of the most popular websites in the world, with over 18 billion page views per month. Encarta? Never heard of it. It was shuttered at the end of 2009. How do we know this? By reading Wikipedia, of course.[1]

It's hard not to be engaged and compelled by Pink's points. Below his talk on TED.com, there's a link to buy his book. I suspect that of the tens of millions of people who watch the talk, many have clicked through to buy the book because they liked the sample he gave in his talk. I did, and I'm glad I did.

Treat speaking as a sampling exercise.

The Strategic Flip

Pink shrank the wall and built demand. And you can too. It starts with asking the right questions.

Speakers frequently begin their prep by asking what sounds like a good question: What do I want to say? It's not a good question. Instead, try flipping it around and asking: What does my audience need to hear? This strategic reorientation will help you find the nexus of what your audience cares about and the ideas you have to help them.

In some cases, you'll know your topic when you begin planning to speak. In other cases, you won't. In all cases, it's important to begin with the strategic flip to considering your audience's needs. Let's explore some questions that will help you confidently Shrink the Wall.

Theoretical and Equitable versus Practical and Relevant

"Why are you wasting 40 percent of your talk time discussing structures that are not relevant to your audience?" I asked five clients who were speaking to a business audience on the topic of joint venture structures in commercial real estate transactions.

"Well, there are five structures and five of us, so we thought we would split up the time so that each of us could talk about one of the structures for ten minutes," they said.

"But you said two of the five structures are almost never used, and your business audience wants practical solutions, right?" I replied.

"Yes, but we want *them* to know that *we* know that there are five structures," they said, succumbing to the Expert's Paradox.

"Let's do that quickly by showing the five structures on a slide. Explain that the bottom two structures are rarely used, so you won't be addressing them today," I suggested. I also encouraged them to say they would advise their clients if they were in the unusual circumstances where they could benefit from the uncommon approaches.

To Shrink the Wall, ask: What are my audience's business or professional objectives? These are rational needs that people will openly talk about. In my clients' case, their audience wanted practical solutions to get the deal done efficiently and avoid unnecessary taxation.

Once my clients narrowed the focus of their remarks, they reallocated their speaking roles and reinvested the time they would've spent on irrelevant structures by bringing to life the relevant ones with instructive examples drawn from their own experience. Feedback from attendees included, "Engaging and extremely helpful—am glad I came."

Ask: What are my audience's business or professional objectives?

Pure Awesomeness

"I have a talented team. Yet when many have to speak, they get tied up in Gordian knots, lost in wormholes of their own thinking," my client told me from his seat in Silicon Valley. We all get so close to our work that it is tough to separate the knotted wormholes of the stuff *we* love from the things our *audience* really cares about. Steve and Joanna faced a similar challenge. They found the pathway out was through asking wall-shrinking questions.

They had conducted a study on the food and beverage industry in North America. Their findings were set out in a beautifully crafted report. What's next? To present the study, of course. At this stage, many thought leaders make the mistake of presenting the whole study. Every question. Every response. Every beautiful graph. Steve and Joanna didn't.

If the tech industry is the hare, the food and beverage industry is the tortoise. Not a hotbed of disruptive innovations. What are some of its challenges? Mature markets, few retailers with a lot of power, and a need for high-volume sales to compensate for low margins. Not exactly the sector that has the venture capitalists on Sand Hill Road salivating.

Yet Steve and Joanna are excited about the sector, and they were looking forward to presenting their study on the key performance drivers across the industry. They directed their excitement: rather than present all of the data, they focused on the two key attributes of successful food and beverage companies. Let's pause for a moment. If you work in a food and beverage company, it's hard not to be intrigued when you see "the two key attributes." Which two?

After they showed that the largest organizations in the United States have the highest earnings, they explained the first driver: debt. The large, profitable organizations were financed by debt (they showed debt-to-total-capitalization stats). They followed with the second driver: the debt was used to invest in brands, innovation, and acquisitions, not in property, plant, and equipment (they showed PP&E-to-total-capitalization ratios). For the balance of the presentation they illustrated how these large, profitable companies made these investments.

The result? The audience ate it up. "The session was truly outstanding. Congrats to both Jo and Steve—excellent content with a very creative spin. Pure awesomeness," wrote their division head. The pair also got a lead from a food and beverage company in the audience to put a cherry on the awesomeness. And attendees wrote to ask if they could distribute the beautiful report to their colleagues.

Steve and Joanna showed they understood their audience's challenges and limited their "wall" by presenting only two data-supported solutions that addressed them.

Ask: What challenges does my audience face?

The Roller Coaster and the Incline Plane

It's hard to walk into a room of dentists who have a hate on for sugar when they think you sell cotton candy. How do you overcome an erroneous negative bias? John Warrillow figured it out.

"My audience thinks that I'm going to compete with them. I'm not. I'm here to help them," Warrillow, founder of the Value Builder System, said to me. He was preparing to speak to a group of advisors and M&A professionals who help owners sell their business. They felt threatened that Warrillow's company was providing products that would make their services irrelevant. This was not true. Not only was Value Builder not competing with them, but also his company—and his book—could help them.

Warrillow devised a plan. When he spoke, he included stories featuring advisors like those in the audience and their clients, who are business owners. In these vignettes, he made the advisor the hero.

"Many market research firms ride the typical feast-and-famine cash flow cycles. Sell the work, deliver the work, sell the work, deliver the work. It's a tough way to manage your emotions, much less your income statement. This was the conundrum faced by an advisor's client," Warrillow explained. Heads in the crowd nodded as they recognized the problem faced by some of their own clients.

He recounted how the advisor guided an owner to transition her business from one with unpredictable six-figure revenue to a stable and growing nine-figure top line. "The advisor told us her client said, 'I thought cash flow certainty and running a business couldn't coexist. With your advice, I got off the cash flow roller coaster, and I have financial confidence and calmness where I thought none would ever come.'"

Warrillow moved his audience from arms-folded skeptics to believers who placed bulk purchase orders for his book to give to their clients. He won the audience over because he anticipated their bias and addressed it. Biases can be negative or positive, true or false. Find theirs out and prepare for more bulk buyers of your ideas.

Ask: What biases does my audience have about me or my product, service, or idea?

Calibrate to Resonate

If Yo-Yo Ma delivers a guest lecture at Juilliard, he can confidently assume the class knows what a chromatic scale is. But if he were talking to me about the same subject, I'd be tone deaf. Be sure to consider how much background knowledge your audience has on your topic before you speak. If you do, you're increasing the chances you'll hit the right note for your listeners.

Ask: How much background knowledge does my audience have?

Solving for Finite Time

How often have you found yourself saying, "I don't have time..."? You aspire to do more, yet, if you're like most people, you might let another year go by without doing some of the things that are important to you because you don't have enough time. Or so you think.

In her Top 100 talk, "How to Gain Control of Your Free Time," Laura Vanderkam challenged her audience's thinking and gave practical tips for doing more of what's important. Her talk racks up millions of views every year because she provides practical tips that speak to people's aspirations.

Aspirations matter. They include things like belonging, appreciation, recognition, and status. Aspirations can be very personal, so your audience might not openly talk about them. But just because they don't talk about them doesn't mean that you shouldn't consider and address them—directly or indirectly.

Approximately one-quarter of the Top 100 talks are aspirational—titles such as "The Power of Believing That You Can Improve," "The Art of Asking," and "The Surprising Science of Happiness" are just a few. That they are popular isn't surprising. Some of the greatest speeches in history are aspirational, such as Martin Luther King Jr.'s "I Have a Dream," John F. Kennedy's "Man on the Moon," and Winston Churchill's "Their Finest Hour."

Ask: What are my audience's aspirations?

Seven Very Costly Words

As organizations swell in size, so do the volumes of their policies and procedures. Creating policy is easy. Getting compliance is hard. How would you convince a bank to make sure their employees are adhering to their document retention and destruction policy? One savvy litigator I coached chose to tap the desire of fear avoidance when he spoke to in-house counsel and chief risk officers in financial institutions.

"'ATHM is such a piece of crap!' These seven words cost Merrill Lynch $100 million," the trial lawyer said, pointing to the quote on a slide. "These words were discovered to have been written in an email by a Merrill analyst at the time he published a piece explaining why the turd of a stock was rated a 'buy.'"[2]

The litigator had the bankers' attention. The desire to avoid a $100 million fine is motivating. And so is the deeper need to avoid public embarrassment. No one wants to be associated with headlines like the ones that came out after the ATHM disclosure. Now that they were moved to act, the litigator armed the audience with tactics to enhance document destruction compliance and implementation tips.

Ask: What are my audience's fears—things they might only disclose to a close confidant?

Winning More with Less

Many of my clients have told me over the years that they want to be more concise. Some of them can't help but elaborate for a few minutes about how concise they want to be. Shrinking the Wall helps you omit swaths of detail that your audience doesn't need to hear. It can also help you win more work.

"Flip through these," said Adele as she pushed a stack of proposals across the table to me. We were sitting in her corner office, which was equipped with a meeting table, suggesting she has so many meetings that it isn't a good use of her time to wander the halls to other boardrooms. People come to her. She'd issued a request for proposal for a significant matter, and five firms had responded.

"What's the first thing you notice?" she asked as I thumbed through them.

"Each is about an inch thick, except one," I said as I pulled the thinner one out from the deck.

"The thinner one is the only proposal I read. It was written for me. The others were boilerplate. If I wanted to read boilerplate, I'd visit their websites," she muttered below her breath.

I cannot give you the formula for success, but I can give you the formula for failure: try to please everybody.

HERBERT BAYARD SWOPE, FIRST RECIPIENT OF THE PULITZER PRIZE

I could see she'd underlined and dog-eared the tailored proposal. "This reminds me of one of those quotes from Ben Franklin or Mark Twain, 'I would have written you a shorter letter if I had more time,'" I said.

"She spent the time—this provider was the only one who called me to discuss the RFP and my needs. It shows. She's outlined exactly what I need, and I'm going to retain her."

Say more of the right things and bypass the boilerplate to stand out.

The Second Filter Set

Shrinking the Wall is a two-step exercise: determine what the audience needs to hear—outlined above—and then consider your communication objectives, which we'll look at now.

Polishing to What End?

Sometimes clients tell me their content is ready and they just want my help to work on the polish. Before we begin the rehearsal, I always ask, "What do you want your audience to do as a result of listening to you?" The most common response is, "Huh ... I hadn't thought about that." These are seasoned, experienced professionals, so I used to be surprised by their answer. After reflecting further on my question, most proceed to reverse engineer an answer based on what they've drafted. A more strategic approach is to answer the question *before* you build your content.

"Hire me," is the second most common response I get, after "Huh ..." It's what I heard from Kevin before he rehearsed a presentation with me on doing distressed M&A deals. "Have you ever done any of these types of deals?" I asked after he ran through the content. He said he had. "Well, you'd never know," I replied.

Kevin was an imposing figure, casting a large shadow on account of his six-foot-four frame and the confidence earned from decades of advising on billion-dollar transactions. His pre-lined brow furrowed further, suggesting he didn't know what I meant.

"You sound like an intelligent academic. Why don't you talk about at least one of the deals you've worked on to illustrate the importance of timing or a negotiation tactic?" He did. And it made all the difference.

At the end of his talk, a client who was in the audience approached him. "We've been working together for decades,

Kevin. I had no idea you'd done these types of deals before. We're about to do one and I was going to give the file to another advisor. It's yours if you want it." He did.

If you want your speaking to help you win work, your audience needs to know you're not just well studied on the topic—let them know you've got experience using your approach to help others achieve successful outcomes. Even if you're not overtly selling, at some point you will want an audience to do something differently. In both cases, it's handy to be clear on what that looks like before you craft your content.

Ask: What do I want my audience to do as a result of listening to me? What do they need to know to be inspired to do the things I want them to do?

Changing Your Approach to Change

If you've ever tried to lead a team through change, you know that it is a tough task. So I was surprised to hear Luke, the head of talent at one of the Big Four, say, "Change management is easy." With that bold statement, he had my attention as he held court with four or five people who were taking a break during one of their colleagues' rehearsals at the King Edward Hotel in downtown Toronto.

Luke has a thick helmet of gray hair and round red cheeks that appear to have been buttressed by a few steaks over the years. "You just have to make the status quo sufficiently uncomfortable," he said as he held out his left hand and wriggled his fingers skyward, "and propose an alternative that's sufficiently attractive," he continued as he mirrored the gesture with his right hand, "that people move from the current to the desired place," he finished, punctuating with his left and right hands.

How do you make people feel sufficiently uncomfortable? Celebrity chef and food activist Jamie Oliver knows.

He combines stats and stories. In February 2010 he won the TED Prize: "a cash award ... that's given annually to a forward-thinking individual with a fresh, bold vision for sparking global change."[3] It comes with the opportunity to speak on the main stage.

When Oliver did, with "Teach Every Child about Food," he paced back to the data on the screen behind him, which showed that the top killers in America were diet-related diseases, and strode forward to the audience to confront them: "We, the adults of the last four generations, have blessed our children with the destiny of a shorter lifespan than their own parents." He explained that the life expectancy of the audience's children was ten years less than their own because of the food that surrounds them.

With his plaid shirtsleeves rolled and his hair scrambled high, Oliver didn't relent and told the audience that two-thirds of the those in the room—in America—are obese. This is not a message this global, jet-setting crowd expected or wanted to hear. But he is committed to starting a food revolution, and he was determined to move this high-powered audience to take action.

Stats alone don't evoke feelings the way hearing about real people does. Oliver put a human face on the massive tragedy by showing a video of himself speaking to his friend Stacy Edwards, a mother of two in Huntington, West Virginia. "Stacy does her best ... She was never taught to cook at home or at school. The family's obese. Justin here, twelve years old, he's 350 pounds. He gets bullied, for God's sake," said Oliver, now speaking and moving faster, his voice a blend of concern, anger, and conviction. He pointed back to the screen, at a picture of her four-year-old daughter Katie, who was already obese even before starting primary school.

Oliver then showed a clip of him sitting with Stacy at the Edwards's kitchen table, which was loaded with a mound of the food they eat weekly: pepperoni pizzas, hot dogs, French fries, fried chicken, pancakes... "I want my kids to succeed in life, and this isn't going to get them there. I'm killing them," Edwards says as she cries. Oliver puts his hand on her shoulder. "Yes, you are. But we can stop that," he reassures her.

Oliver's mission is not to lecture, condescend, or demean. His sights are set on saving lives through educating students about food and inspiring families to cook again, all to fight obesity. As he closed, he moved the room to their feet, an impossible feat without emotion front and center.

If you want to move people, emotion is *the* lever. Oliver knows it's essential to tap it if you want people to join your revolution—or just join you for dinner.

Ask: How do I want my audience to feel during and after my talk?

SHRINKING THE WALL is important when you're preparing to speak in any situation. Arguably it's even more critical when speaking online, when it's even easier for your audience to be distracted and disengage.

Now that you've confidently narrowed your focus, it's time to build your content, which we will look at next.

2

CREATE AN IDEA QUIVER

IF YOU WANT to move the room, you need to be in the room. The most common thing that will pull you out of the room? Your notes. You may be tempted to write down all of your important ideas and bring them with you into the room. When you are under pressure, you may subconsciously decide to put your notes to good use—that is what they are for, after all. Yet, as we have seen with the monotonous technical speaker who read simple definitions and even his name, this approach is fraught with risk. Notes aren't the problem, but how we use them can be.

How do you organize your content and use notes to make it easier to remember what you want to say? Create an Idea Quiver.

Imagine trying to ride a horse while carrying a fistful of arrows in one hand and a bow and the reins in the other, galloping in pursuit of some prey. That's a tough task for all but the best riders. For the rest of us, using a container to carry the arrows—a quiver—could make the difference between failure and feeding your family. You can benefit from having a quiver to organize your ideas, remember them easily, and quickly retrieve them if you need to during your talks.

The Idea Quiver includes a series of compartments. Let's explore what they are and what you might put in them.

Commanding Opening

How would you introduce a talk on the progress of gender diversity on public company boards? This was a question Alison had to answer in the spring of 2018. She is a marketing exec who has a delightful blend of gravitas, glamor—including a red carpet-worthy footwear collection—and self-described goofiness. But when it comes to contributing to the advancement of women to more leadership roles, she doesn't joke around. Under her leadership, Alison's firm did a series of studies to track the progress of gender diversity on boards in various sectors and geographies across the country. She was giving a talk on the report, and she wanted to start strong.

"I was chatting with a friend recently who was in an audience on a winter morning in 1992. He and his business school classmates had the opportunity to listen to a woman who was a director of one of the most prominent public companies in Canada," Alison said to a packed house of senior and striving women. "During the Q&A, someone asked the director, 'How will we know when we are making progress with women in leadership roles?' Without hesitation, she said, 'When people stop asking me what it's like to be a woman director for a publicly traded company and start asking me what it's like to be a director.'"

On its face, Alison's lead-in doesn't appear to be overly noteworthy, but it is. It allowed Alison to begin conversationally and build anticipation from her first sentence. Most people don't start conversationally, and few build anticipation from the get-go.

Picture how most people do start. They read perfunctory points from notes: thank you for the opportunity to speak; thank you for the kind introduction; it's a pleasure to be here; a few housekeeping details; lots to cover so let's dive in … Is there anything wrong with this approach? No. Is it a missed opportunity to begin with power? You bet.

A commanding opening checks the following boxes: it allows you to be in the room (it encourages you to speak conversationally while looking at your audience, not your notes); it builds anticipation for your talk; and it is relevant to your purpose. What makes your intro commanding is the *combination* of these elements. It's not about having jaw-dropping content, which is nice but not necessary.

The Top 100 use a variety of approaches in their openings. Here's a summary to help get you on your way to making a strong start.

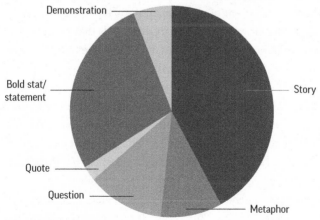

OPENING DEVICE: TOP 100 TED TALKS

Demonstration

Bold stat/ statement

Quote

Question

Story

Metaphor

It's important that the end of the commanding opening includes a link to connect it to the next compartment, the statement of purpose. For Alison, she responded to the question put to the director by saying, "There has been progress. That director is now the chair of the board, for starters. Today I want to talk about the progress that our study reveals that we are—and are not—making and what we can do to continue to support the advancement of women on boards."

You will find it's easier to come up with a great intro if you prepare it last. You'll be clearer on what you are introducing—so your intro will be relevant—and you will reduce the likelihood of getting writer's block.

Begin by starting conversationally, in the room, and building anticipation for the rest of your talk.

Statement of Purpose

This is self-defined: What's your talk about? This is the journey you are promising to take your audience on.

Alison's statement of purpose above was, "Today I want to talk about the progress that our study reveals that we are—and are not—making and what we can do to continue to support the advancement of women on boards."

On January 9, 2007, Steve Jobs introduced Apple's most transformative product yet at Macworld in San Francisco. In fact, in his intro, he told the audience he was going to introduce three revolutionary products. The audience applauded, whistled, and cheered as he announced each: a widescreen iPod with touch controls, a revolutionary mobile phone, and a breakthrough internet communications device. "These are not three separate devices. This is one device. And we are calling it iPhone." After another eruption of applause, Jobs stated his purpose, "Today, Apple is going to reinvent the phone, and here it is."[1]

Ironically, it's his invention that's had the unintended consequence of creating a need for us to learn how to become better conversationalists. Journalist Celeste Headlee reinforces this point before stating the purpose of her Top 100 talk, "10 Ways to Have a Better Conversation": "So I'd like to spend the next ten minutes or so teaching you how to talk and how to listen."

State your purpose.

Essential Messages

Essential messages provide a roadmap that is the frame for your talk—how you're going to achieve the objectives you set out for your remarks. You don't need to announce your roadmap at the beginning, but it is imperative that *you* know what it is.

In Sheryl Sandberg's Top 100 talk, "Why We Have Too Few Women Leaders," she set out her essential messages clearly at the beginning. "My talk today is about what the messages are if you do want [women] to stay in the workforce, and I think there are three. One, sit at the table. Two, make your partner a real partner. And three, don't leave before you leave. Number one: sit at the table..."

Determining the right essential messages is harder than you might think. Expect some tinkering and recasting as you prepare. It's often helpful to ask yourself "why?" or "how?" at the end of the statement of purpose to take your first cut at figuring out your essential messages.

For instance, let's say I want to give a short talk to encourage you to consider taking up windsurfing. Why windsurf?

1   It's exhilarating to skim across the water.
2   It allows you to enjoy the beauty of nature in a new way.
3   It's rewarding because it's challenging.

Notice how these essential messages are mutually exclusive. Overlapping essential messages will cloud your communication. For example, if you are encouraging people to dine with friends more frequently, you might give the following reasons: it encourages relationships; it fosters friendships; and you can get to know each other better. These aren't discrete messages, though, so the communication is muddy.

If your goal is to persuade people, put your most compelling point first. The sooner you have your audience agree with you, the better. I really would love you to learn to windsurf, and I think if I elaborate on exhilaration, I'll have my best shot at getting you on a board.

The exception to putting your most compelling point first is if your idea needs to be explained in a logical progression if it's to be understood. I have been an assistant baseball coach for my son's team for five years. In teaching skills to the boys, I have learned the importance of explaining steps in the proper sequence. For instance, to hit with more power, establish your athletic stance, then load, then drive your hips... There's no point in driving your hips if you haven't established your athletic stance. The same is likely true if you're explaining how asset-backed securities can be used to raise more capital.

How Many Essential Messages Should You Include?

Whenever you see a speaker with an exhaustive agenda, it's usually a signal that they didn't Shrink the Wall. As a starting

point, you might aim to have three or four essential messages—
more and you'll lose the audience.

Having three points is timeless, for good reason. There are
endless proven three-point structures, including the simplest
storytelling arc of beginning, middle, and end. From an early
age we were exposed to ideas organized in trios, such as big,
bigger, biggest. There's a nice cadence to a series of three. A
two-point list often feels incomplete. Notice that people who
have a two-point list try to turn it into three by adding "et cet-
era" or "and so on."

Bryan Stevenson is a lawyer, a social justice activist, and the
founder of the Equal Justice Initiative. He has gained international acclaim for his work challenging bias against the poor
and minorities in the criminal justice system. Stevenson is
an inspiring person and an intelligent, engaging speaker who
has a lot to teach us. What he accomplishes in four points is
remarkable.

In his talk, "You Don't Create Justice by Doing What Is
Comfortable," as part of the Google Zeitgeist series featuring
people who are changing the world, he begins by using stats
to confront us with the size of the problem and explain why
we should care about inequality and injustice. Then he out-
lines the four things the audience can do to curb the troubling
trends and make change in the world: get proximate to the
problem, change the narrative, be hopeful, and do uncomfortable things.

Your essential messages don't need to be understood on
their own, without elaboration. Stevenson's aren't all understandable at first glance—we don't know what "get proximate
to the problem" means yet, but we will.

Can you have five essential messages? Possibly. Top 100
speaker Julian Treasure gave five simple exercises to improve
listening in his "5 Ways to Listen Better."[2] Yet the ratio of his

essential messages to support for them gets skewed to the point where his ideas seem thin and less memorable.

I call them "essential" for a reason. Is it essential you speak to these points to achieve your objectives? If the answer is yes and you're left with six or more essential messages, try to roll them up into some higher-order structure, and then unpack them as you speak like Russian matryoshka dolls, with smaller dolls nested in bigger ones.

Should You Announce Your Roadmap?

Once you have your essential messages to frame your remarks, you may be wondering if you should tell your audience what your messages are up front or announce them as you go. Here are some pros for enumerating your essential messages:

Clarity—It will make it easier for your audience to anticipate where you're going to take them and understand the scaffolding of your broader story. The more complex your talk, the more helpful your structure will be.

Cadence—If you pause after the numerals, it will prompt you to slow down. Most people speak too quickly at the beginning of their talks because they have some nervous energy. Put the brakes on by pausing after the numerals.

Concision—When you enumerate, you're more inclined to plan the content that will follow. This planning encourages you to be more concise.

Conviction—The act of enumerating physically by snapping out the right number of digits will prompt you to speak with more conviction and authority. Try it.

Confidence—You will be more confident in your ability to remember what you want to say.

And all of the above are conducive to allowing you to engender confidence in your listener. Win/win. Yet nothing is perfect, and there are some downsides to enumerating a roadmap. It can make you sound very formal—I wouldn't enumerate why your niece is an incredible young woman when toasting her at her wedding. There is a risk that enumerating can make your talk seem formulaic. Weak content combined with a transparent structure may come across like amateur hour. If you are one of a series of speakers at an event and all the speakers enumerate roadmaps, a whiff of sausage-making might slip into the room, which may explain why just under one-quarter of the Top 100 TED talks have a transparent structure like Sandberg's.

If your content is great, the audience won't notice your structure or will appreciate knowing your framework so they can more easily digest your content as it comes. The best restaurants in the world still divide their menus into appetizers, entrées, and dessert. What makes dining remarkable is the food and the experience, not the transparent organization of the menu items. If you start by being in the room, sounding conversational, and building anticipation for your talk, the audience will be keen to go on the journey with you, with or without an enumerated roadmap.

Frame your talk with essential messages.

Power Messages to Build Support and Proof

This is such an important part that I've dedicated the entire next chapter to it. Here you will elaborate on your essential messages. Bryan Stevenson does so by using one major story to illustrate the importance of each of his four core solutions. It's the combination of his solutions and the stories that makes him a powerful speaker who brings the audience to their feet. If you watch only one talk as a result of reading this book, make it his Google Zeitgeist talk. His important message is both masterfully constructed and powerfully delivered.

Connect the Compartments

Segues are the connective tissue that links together your mutually exclusive essential messages.

In my windsurfing example, after my last point under the windsurfing-is-exhilarating section, I could say, "The sensation of skimming across the water is exhilarating on its own. It's even more exhilarating when you do it in a stunning location, which is the next thing I am going to talk about..."

Segues are helpful, but not always necessary. Sometimes an abrupt change of subtopic is a good way to snap the audience's attention back. If you have chosen to enumerate your sections, then as you finish one you can simply announce the next enumerated section, as Stevenson did: "The fourth thing we have to do—and this is the hard one—is that we have to do uncomfortable things."

If your segues are too smooth and frequent, there's a risk that you may come off as slick. To avoid this, use segues selectively.

Pulling It Together

What are the top three or four things you really want your audience to take away from your presentation? Your answer to this question will set you up with a helpful summary. You can signal you are winding things up with simple phrases such as, "Let me wrap things up," "To sum up," "In closing," or "If you were to take away only a few things from my talk, here are the most important ones..."

If you plan to take questions at the end of your talk, before using one of these phrases, you might say, "Before I open the floor to questions..." This will prompt those in your audience inclined to ask questions to get ready. Giving them advance warning will reduce the potential for a long, awkward pause when you do open the floor for questions. We will cover Q&A in more detail later.

If you're speaking on a light topic for a short period of time, you can skip the summary. But if you're speaking on a technical topic for a longer stint, a summary is helpful, but it is used less often than you'd think. Too often people don't have enough time to summarize because they've been too busy being comprehensive—they have not shrank the wall. But you're not going to do that.

Remind your audience of your top takeaways when giving long, technical talks.

Closing with Power

Remember Alison, who started her progress-of-women-on-boards talk by referencing the question about what it's like to be a woman director? She closed by putting an image of the cover of the April 3, 2017, *New Yorker* up on the screen and asking the audience, "What are we looking at here?"[3]

"A bunch of surgeons," someone called out. "Yes," said Alison, turning back to look at the image. "What else do you notice?" The cover illustration showed four surgeons wearing masks and scrub caps gazing down as though you are looking up at them from the operating table. The French artist Malika Favre who created it had said, "I tried to capture that feeling of people watching you lose consciousness."[4]

"All four of the surgeons are women," someone else said.

"Yes, they are. The theme for the magazine issue was medicine and health, not gender," said Alison. "Four surgeons, all of whom are women, in an issue that had nothing to do with gender. I think the director I mentioned would agree that this is progress. Many surgeons do, and found the cover to be a cause for celebration. Dr. Nancy Baxter, chief of general surgery at St. Michael's Hospital in Toronto, said, 'Seeing myself on the cover of *The New Yorker* as something normative is amazing.' She and thousands of female surgeons around the world replicated the photo and posted it on social media using the hashtag #ILookLikeASurgeon."[5]

With this image, Alison bookended her talk by tying together her introduction with her close. This approach adds symmetry and gives the audience a sense of closure, particularly if you end up answering a question that you posed off the top, as she did.

Your close is a great time to re-examine your answer to the question, "What do you want your audience to do as result of listening to you?" More often than not you might come right out and make an ask of your audience. Forty percent of the Top 100 speakers close with a call to action, and you can too. In some cases, the call can be explicit, like, "Meditate for ten minutes a day."

Sometimes it's more powerful to be less direct. Rather than having them feel as if they are being sold to, you might give your audience the power to buy into your offering, as Top 100 presenter Andy Puddicombe did in his talk, "All It Takes Is 10 Mindful Minutes." "That's the potential of meditation, of mindfulness," he continued. "You don't have to burn any incense, and you definitely don't have to sit on the floor. All you need to do is to take ten minutes out a day to step back, to familiarize yourself with the present moment, so that you get to experience a greater sense of focus, calm, and clarity in your life."

Of course, there are a range of approaches you could take to close your remarks. Here's a summary of the ones used by the Top 100.

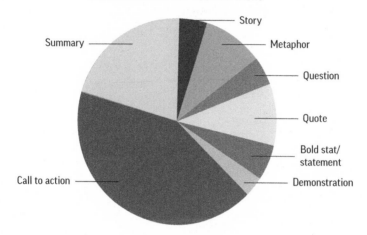

CLOSING DEVICE: TOP 100 TED TALKS

Be the Close

Whatever you do, make sure that you close—not a video, *you*. You don't want to cede the floor to a screen. Take full advantage of your last opportunity to look at your audience and tell them what you think and ask them to take action. You could use a video in the first part of your close, but make sure there is something important left for you to say for the rest of your close.

In my windsurfing example, I could show you a video of a windsurfer in Lac Bay, Bonaire. The shot would pan from the white sandy beach to turquoise tropical water until a beginner sailor glides into the frame. The gleeful pride on her face would say, "Woohoo, I'm doing it!" without me needing to say anything. Then I would tell you that one of life's great rewards is making progress learning a skill and ask, "When was the last time you learned something so satisfying, surrounded by so much beauty?" I could end there or encourage you to visit ABK Boardsports.com to spark ideas about where in the world you might travel and experience feeling even more alive. (I'm not an affiliate marketer. I'm just a passionate windsurfer...)

Close with symmetry and clarity.

3

ADD POWER
MESSAGES

Balcony Heroes

Imagine you've been the president of the United States for seven years. During this time, the country has experienced a housing crisis, a great recession, and an eventual recovery. Now you have the chance to talk about the state of the nation to millions of TV viewers. How would you do it?

A logical approach would be to cite data such as jobs grown, debts repaid, and consumer confidence gained. This data is important. But big numbers are abstract, and citing a series of them is dry and boring. To make your points relatable, you might talk instead about Rebekah and Ben Erler of Minneapolis. That's what President Obama did.

During his 2015 State of the Union address, he explained that seven years earlier the Erlers had been newlyweds and new parents. When the financial crisis hit, Ben's construction work dried up, while Rebekah waited tables and enrolled in community college funded by student loans. They scrimped and sacrificed, and slowly things improved. She got a better job and earned a raise, and Ben found work in construction again. They had a second child. She wrote the president and told him, "It is amazing what you can bounce back from when you have to . . . We are a strong, tight-knit family who has made it through some very, very hard times."

The president repeated that last line, "We are a strong, tight-knit family who has made it through some very, very hard times." He went on to say:

> America, Rebekah and Ben's story is our story. They represent the millions who've worked hard, and scrimped, and sacrificed, and retooled. You are the reason that I ran for this office. You are the people I was thinking of six years ago today, in the darkest months of the crisis, when I stood on the steps of this Capitol and promised we would rebuild our economy on a new foundation. And it has been your resilience, your effort that has made it possible for our country to emerge stronger.[1]

Rebekah and Ben were present during his address, Rebekah sitting next to the first lady in the balcony of Congress. The Erlers are Balcony Heroes: real, relatable, and representative examples of countless others. You might use Balcony Heroes too.

As a subject matter expert, you probably spend most of your time talking about abstract, complex concepts. Yet you probably also know how hard it is to engage an audience for a sustained period of time when the material you're talking about is dry and conceptual. Balcony Heroes can bring your ideas alive and make them engaging and compelling.

Ronald Reagan was the first president to use Balcony Heroes in the flesh as a rhetorical approach in his first State of the Union (SOTU) address.[2] Every year, the president uses this address to tell a joint session of Congress—and millions of Americans watching on TV—about the progress of the nation and his party's legislative plans for the coming year. Imagine how tough it must be to summarize a country's work in an hour.

Here's a summary of what Reagan covered in his inaugural SOTU—find the one thing that stands out: the economy, taxes, government spending, foreign policy, the constitution, the military, civil rights, and Lenny Skutnik. Wait, Lenny who? Reagan explained:

> Just two weeks ago, in the midst of a terrible tragedy on the Potomac, we saw again the spirit of American heroism at its finest—the heroism of dedicated rescue workers saving [plane] crash victims from icy waters. And we saw the heroism of one of our young government employees, Lenny Skutnik, who, when he saw a woman lose her grip on the helicopter line, dived into the water and dragged her to safety.[3]

At this point, the House erupted in a forty-second standing ovation for Skutnik, who was seated in the House balcony beside First Lady Nancy Reagan. During the ovation, Reagan looked at the gray-suited Skutnik and saluted him. Then the president extrapolated:

> And then there are countless, quiet, everyday heroes of American life—parents who sacrifice long and hard so their children will know a better life than they've known; church and civic volunteers who help to feed, clothe, nurse, and teach the needy; millions who've made our nation and our nation's destiny so very special—unsung heroes who may not have realized their own dreams themselves but then who reinvest those dreams in their children. Don't let anyone tell you that America's best days are behind her, that

the American spirit has been vanquished. We've seen it triumph too often in our lives to stop believing in it now.

How many presidents have had heroes in the balcony since Reagan's 1982 SOTU? Every single one. Why? They work.

The president has some of the best speechwriters in the world working on the SOTU address. If there was a better way to engage the audience, they would swap out the heroes and sub in the better approach. But they don't.

My question for you: Are you using Balcony Heroes as often as you could? I suspect not. This is not a comment about you, but it reflects my experience. I have coached countless leaders since 1998, and when I first see a speaker's plan, it's almost always bereft of Balcony Heroes.

Now you may be thinking, "Wait a second—I'm an expert talking about weighty matters, but I'm not the president of the United States. At least not yet. I don't talk about military feats, unemployment rates, or policy plans. How can I use Balcony Heroes?"

Talk about how your work affects people. What do people ask you? What concerns do they disclose? What aspirations are they striving to achieve? Talk about these. Humanize your work by explaining how you help people answer these questions, address their concerns, and achieve their bigger and brighter futures.

Your Balcony Heroes don't need to be in the room—they don't have to be actual heroes. But they do need to be real, relatable people so your listeners grasp the impact you have. Illustrate with one person, one Balcony Hero, then extrapolate to include more people. When you do, you will see your audience's eyes light up and spirits rise—and who knows, they may even get up on their feet.

Talk about real, representative people and then extrapolate.

Balcony Heroes are powerful messages. To understand what makes messages powerful, let's turn to Seanna Millar.

A Pound of Butter

Seanna Millar doesn't just pitch for a living, she pitches to save lives. "I've seen a baby the size of a pound of butter that would fit in the palm of my hand," she said, cupping her hands around a tiny, invisible package. "She was in the neonatal intensive care unit—the NICU—of our hospital. Now picture four premature babies and their families housed in one room at the hospital, because our NICU doesn't have space for private rooms. Each child's 180-square-foot part of the room is sectioned with red duct tape on the floor," she explained as she portioned the space around her with her arms.

Having so many vulnerable babies in close quarters presents all kinds of challenges and complications. Millar continued, "It's hard enough for many new mothers to breastfeed their children in the privacy of their own homes. Imagine trying to do that with three other families just feet away from you. It's stressful and exhausting." She let the point sit for a few seconds before adding, "When we are exhausted, we are more susceptible to getting sick. If a mom gets sick, she is told that she has to go home and cannot visit her own child for fear of making the other babies in the room sick. Imagine if that mom was you."

Seanna had now pulled the room into a collective presence. She slowed down next. "Or, in the worst case, imagine as a parent needing to have one of the most difficult conversations you could ever have—saying goodbye to your child forever—when other families are steps away from you."

She's a professional fundraiser who works for the SickKids Foundation, the fundraising arm of SickKids, a world-renowned pediatric teaching hospital in Toronto. It recently launched a campaign to raise $1.5 billion to build a new hospital, fund research, and help doctors and nurses around the world deliver better care. This is the largest hospital fundraising campaign in Canadian history. I coached the hospital executives and foundation leaders with their campaign pitch.

Pitching is not simply about making an emotive appeal. You also need to be prepared to reinforce the case in a rational way, such as by citing best practices at leading pediatric hospitals and comparing them to the current and proposed ones at Sick-Kids. Millar does all this. And she raises millions.

She uses Power Messages, and you can too. They evoke powerful reactions from people, including, "That's terrible. That is unacceptable. We must do better. What can I do to help?" Power Messages can also elicit positive reactions, such as, "That's impressive," "That's exactly what I need," and "I want that too!"

Use Power Messages to evoke strong, desired reactions.

Balcony Heroes are one type of Power Message. We are going to cover others that you'll want to selectively use, whether you're pitching for millions to save lives or making your case on day-to-day matters.

Examples

How Much Impact Could You Have with Three Words and Three Circles?

Quick, how many present-day advertisers can you name? I'm not talking about the dead-guy masthead monikers like Ogilvy or McCann. And, no, Don Draper doesn't count. Living, working advertisers.

Here is one that you may have heard of, but not because of his work in advertising. He gave a talk where he drew three circles and wrote three words on a flip chart in a presentation in Puget Sound. The talk, "How Great Leaders Inspire Action," was recorded and posted online. It's now been viewed over 50 million times and translated into forty-seven languages. Why? Because he combined a simple, helpful construct with concrete, relatable, and inspiring examples. In the middle circle he wrote, "Why," as in, "Why do you do what you do?" The next circle was "How" (do you do what you do?) and then finally "What" (do you do?). To clarify what the circles represented, he explained it in terms of an example everyone can understand: Apple.

He is Simon Sinek. Sinek has gone on to write a series of bestselling books, and he speaks about leadership to tens of thousands of people a year for tens of thousands of dollars per talk. Take away the examples, though, and you also take away his TED talk's impact—and Sinek's far-reaching influence on millions of people, from military leaders to leading managers of global brands to tier-one think tanks.

Close the Gap

You may be thinking, "Yes, I get it. I know to use examples." But guess what? If you're like most of my intelligent and accomplished speakers, you probably don't. The best ones do.

How many examples do you think the Top 100 use in a typical eighteen-minute talk? I have asked countless people this question, and their response is typically in the range of three to five. Wrong. The answer is considerably higher: eighteen. One example every minute.

Some of the Top 100 speakers take several minutes to explain one example, while others can bang out three examples in less than three seconds. In my assessment, this doesn't matter—every example counts, regardless of how long it takes to cover. Let's not confuse quantity with quality—I'm just trying to set the baseline to compare what I typically see when professionals have an opportunity to talk about their work.

How many examples do you think my clients use in a similar eighteen-minute time frame? These are intelligent, accomplished strategic advisors and business leaders. When I see the first draft, the answer is approaching zero. There's a gap that likely exists between your practice and best practice. Why don't people use more examples? They are too caught up in being comprehensive because they didn't Shrink the Wall. After you shrink yours, find ways to bring your remaining ideas alive with examples. You likely have some work to do here, so to spark some ideas and show some additional benefits, let's look at some examples of examples—a bit meta, I know.

Hitch Your Organization to a Star

Here's a fun challenge. Think about a conceptual construct that your colleagues or clients find to be helpful. Sketch it out. Maybe it is a 2 × 2 matrix that intersects high- and low-market share on the y-axis and high- and low-market growth rate on the x-axis. If you don't recognize it, this is the Boston Consulting Group's famous stars-and-dogs growth share matrix.[4]

Now prepare concrete, relatable, and inspiring examples to animate the concept. Next challenge: explain the concept to somebody *without* using the examples. Notice how your audience responds. Then add the examples and contrast the audience's response.

Ask a dozen business leaders if they know the BCG stars-and-dogs matrix. Many will. Then ask them to name any other construct from any other leading consulting firm. Many won't be able to. BCG's stars-and-dogs matrix has proven to be a powerful way to segment products and a memorable way to distinguish the firm in the market.

Use examples to illustrate constructs and frameworks.

Attention Rupture or Rapture?

I saw Allan, the head of a $14 billion national retailer, speak at a luncheon club. It was hosted in a large ballroom replete with Doric columns, where past speakers have included heads of state, tech titans, and royalty.

After the head table parade and a traditional toast, Allan stood in his crisp blue suit and with boyish enthusiasm began to explain that the company's data helps them really know Canadians and provide the right products to them. Talking analytics alone isn't typically the recipe to audience rapture. So he went on to ask, "What percentage of Canadians do you think shoot left or right in hockey? For many years, our gut instinct told us it was somewhere down the middle. But now we know that it's actually 56 left- to 44 right-hand, and it's not split the same across the country. Only 25 percent of people in the Maritimes shoot left, and it's the opposite in British Columbia. Part of having the right products is having the right assortment and the right inventory in the right stores. Our analytics make sure we have the right mix of sticks in our stores across the country." Fitting to use a hockey stick example for a quintessentially Canadian retailer.

Notice the concreteness of Allan's example. He doesn't just talk about the "right products," he talks about left- and right-shot hockey sticks. He doesn't mention jurisdictions in the generic, he cites the Maritimes and British Columbia. These descriptions are specific, vivid, and memorable.

This is not about dumbing it down. It's about understanding the core idea and explaining it without jargon, or, as I read recently, "jargon monoxide."[5] How would you explain how the economy works? Imagine how easy it would be to lose your audience. Ray Dalio is the founder of Bridgewater Associates, the largest hedge fund in the world. He's written a bestselling book, *Principles*. And he's explained how the economy works in a thirty-minute video, "How the Economic Machine Works."[6] In it, he explains the three things that drive the economy and illustrates them with examples such as buying TVs and tractors on credit. As of today, as I'm writing this, it's been viewed over 23 million times—perhaps a few more than your old economics professor's videos.

Use examples to make the abstract concrete.

Who Do You Want in the Flight Deck?

If the examples you use are drawn from your work, you will further enhance your credibility. Who would you rather pilot your plane: an aeronautical engineer with a couple of doctorates and a pilot's license or Captain "Sully" (Chesley Sullenberger), the former Air Force fighter pilot who safely landed an Airbus A320 with 155 passengers on the Hudson River after both of the plane's engines were disabled by a bird strike? Captain Sully has experience that builds confidence. Examples inspired by your work allow you to subtly showcase your experience and engender confidence in your capabilities.

When I began my career as a presentation coach, I was twenty-seven years old—and I looked like I was seventeen. When I spoke with business leaders about my work back then, they would often make positive, noncommittal, and politely dismissive comments like, "Oh, that's great. I took a speech course thirty-three years ago in undergrad and it was terrific." When these same people found out about the caliber of my clientele and the results that they enjoyed—as revealed through examples—they would unfold their arms, lean in, and say, "Actually, can you help me out with a talk…?"

I am not suggesting that you gratuitously drop names or breach confidentiality. You can selectively illustrate your ideas to add clarity and subtly deepen credibility without seeming self-satisfied or being unprofessional (I will address confidentiality later).

Use examples to establish credibility and trust.

A Sticky Strike

A waste management expert was talking on the radio about "wish cycling": when consumers put things in their blue bin that they don't have the heart to throw out but don't want to keep. The radio host asked, "Like what?" The garbage guru said, "Well, last week we pulled out a ten-pin bowling ball from someone's blue bin. We can't recycle that." I've not written or talked about wish cycling since. I didn't write it down. But the bowling ball made it clear and indelible—maybe because I thought it would be cool to wear bowling shoes in high school. (I tried, and it wasn't.)

The idea of using examples is simple. In practice, most people don't use them or are a long way from an example a minute. Add more of them to your speaking, and more people will appreciate the value of your ideas—and you'll build more demand for your capabilities.

Use examples to make concepts understandable and memorable.

Storytelling

A Hug in the Lobby

How many times have you asked someone who's struggling, "Is there anything I can do?" I don't ask that question anymore because of what I learned from watching Sheryl Sandberg speak with Ellen DeGeneres. They were in angled white leather chairs on the bright palm-treed set of *The Ellen DeGeneres Show*.[7]

Sheryl was talking about losing her husband Dave while on vacation in Mexico and having to tell their seven- and ten-year-old children that they were never going to see their father again.

Ellen asked her what we should and should not say to people when they are grieving. Sheryl explained that she used to ask others if there was anything she could do. While her offer was sincere, she's come to realize it shifts the burden to the person you're trying to help—the onus is on them to come up with the idea. When she was asked this question, she told Ellen, "I didn't know what to say: 'Well, can you make Father's Day disappear, so I don't have to live through it every year?'"

The room was still. Ellen nodded almost imperceptibly, and Sheryl continued, "Instead of offering to do anything, just do something." She then told the story of a friend who had lost a child after many months in hospital. "One of his friends texted him and said, 'I'm in the lobby of the hospital for a hug for the next hour whether you come down or not.' That is powerful."

It is so powerful that it's always stuck with me, and I do my best to act on it every time I see someone struggling. Sheryl Sandberg changed my understanding of my behavior toward those who are grieving. She did it with a story.

Use a story to spark individual change.

A Magnetic Epiphany

Changing individual behavior is hard. Changing at an organizational level is even harder. Steve has been trying to help companies change for the better for decades and is now leading a global management consulting practice.

I sat down with him for a coffee in an Italian eatery that makes you feel like you're in a giant, airy wine cask in the heart of the financial district. His consultant uniform and pristine hair was what you'd expect from someone who uses his engineering and military background to drive efficiency in his clients' companies.

If you want to build a ship, don't drum up the men to go to the forest to gather wood, saw and nail the planks together. Instead teach them with the desire for the sea.
ATTRIBUTED TO ANTOINE DE SAINT-EXUPÉRY

What I didn't expect was for him to say, "I had an epiphany the other day. I was in a meeting where we were talking about the typical barriers to helping organizations transform: lack of executive support, technical uncertainty, no shared vision … It occurred to me that another, more important barrier was almost always missing: story. An overarching, unifying story to rally and inspire organizations."

His eyes lit up as he leaned across his cappuccino and added, "Do you remember that science experiment as a kid when you would scatter iron filings on top of a piece of paper? Then, you'd put a magnet under the page—and what happens? All the filings that had been scattered haphazardly become organized in a pattern. Trying to align filings without a magnet would be monumentally hard. That's like trying to drive transformation without a well-designed story.

"Many organizations are dominated by left-brained, analytical people who obsess over analytics and business process," he continued. "These are important but aren't enough to get us where we want to go. Focusing on designing, living, and communicating compelling stories will do for transformation what no amount of structure, methodology, or data on their own can match."

Steve's observations aren't scattered musings. They're based on hard-won experience from decades in the trenches of advising big companies on large-scale transformations.

Changing an organization's behavior without story is monumentally hard.

Use story to create organizational alignment and drive change.

Story is one of the most powerful levers you can use to move the room. We've seen how it can drive change. Let's quickly look at a few more reasons to tell stories before digging into how to build betters ones using the Story Builder on page 57.

Story Saves Lives

Imagine trying to run a large mining company safely. One that has thousands of employees working twenty-four hours a day, seven days a week, for millions of person-hours every year in an industry that requires heavy equipment and massive machinery to operate. This has been Don Lindsay's job since April 2005, when he became CEO of Teck Resources, which owns or has interests in ten major mines, including Greenhills Operations in Elk Valley, British Columbia.

This is where they lost Terry Twast, a mine rescue captain, while he was operating a bulldozer during a foggy night on October 20, 2005. He mistakenly drove over a bank and fell to the bottom of a pit. This tragedy was a turning point for Teck. "We said enough is enough," Lindsay explained. They decided to implement the Courageous Safety Leadership program.[8]

The program is built with the understanding that strong technical safety programs alone won't create a sustainable culture of safety. "People are complex. We make choices and we make mistakes," says Lindsay. To build a positive safety culture, Teck uses story to personalize the impact that choices made every day on the job have on the lives of other people. People like Toni Foster, mine accountant at their Cardinal River Operations, south of Hinton, Alberta.

She described how her husband, Gordon Foster, suffered a fatal thirty-five-foot fall onto a cement deck, and explained how the loss continues to affect her. "Every day, I drive this highway," she said as she showed a photo of a two-lane highway cutting through the rolling countryside as it heads toward mountains in the distance. "And every day I drive by his grave. And I've got to tell you guys, that hurts. It hurts a lot." She pulled her lips tight to keep more hurt from spilling out and said, "I would give everything I have for one more minute."

She was clear about why she was speaking: "Part of my goal in getting up and sharing this story no matter how much it hurts is I believe we learn from examples." She finished by asking her colleagues to be responsible, to be leaders, and to speak up. Lives at work—and lives of loved ones at home—depend on it.

Since its inception, 17,000 employees and long-term contractors have taken the program. In it, positive-change stories also play an important role. Stories like that of a crane operator mechanic, Jorge Espinoza, working in Teck's open-pit copper cathode mine in Quebrada Blanca, northern Chile.

He determined a 27-ton slab of cement was too heavy to be lifted safely by the 250-ton crane. Some workers wanted to go ahead with the move anyway, but Espinoza refused. "I called my supervisor and explained that given the load table of the crane, this was really high risk." They leased a 350-ton capacity crane and got the job done—safely. "We have a duty to speak up when we see something unsafe," said Espinoza. He is one of countless Courageous Safety Leaders spotlighted by Teck.

"We strongly believe that success builds success; sharing positive stories creates a positive culture," says Lindsay. "Our storytelling approach has had a profound impact." In the last ten years, they've reduced their injury frequency by two-thirds. That's a lot more people going home safely every day.

Personalize loss and celebrate wins with story. Lives may depend on it.

Gum over Grains

It's no secret that the prospect of speaking in important situations creates anxiety for most of us. Much of the anxiety traces back to the fear of forgetting what you want to say: the grains of your content will slip from your brain, and you'll be left speechless and looking foolish. Many mitigate this risk by preparing thoughtful notes and then referring to them. Yet, when they look at their notes, their eyes disengage from the room and their vocal range compresses. Audiences disengage and confidence plummets—theirs and yours.

What's a better approach? Shrink the Wall and then illustrate with story. Stories will stick like pine gum to memory in a way the tiny grains of too many points never will. Shifting your approach to making fewer, stickier points will make your job as speaker easier and the audience's recall better.

Nine years ago, I watched a CEO, Wes, talk to his colleagues about the need to provide service excellence—an important topic that can lend itself to trite exhortations. This wasn't his approach. He doesn't set standards and demand compliance. He knows better—he's a savvy leader who's earned all the wisdom suggested by his thinning, wiry white hair. Wes introduces ideas through story in a way that gives listeners the choice to adopt them as their own; this approach is part of what makes him effective as a leader of a group of driven professionals.

As he stood at the front of the room, he recounted a story of a couple who were checking in to the Ritz-Carlton in New York City. During the check-in, one of the guests whispered to the staff member at the reception desk, "Can I order some champagne and strawberries to my room tomorrow at 4 pm?" He smiled and added, "Oh, and I don't want my girlfriend to know."

The Ritz team member returned the smile, leaned forward, and asked quietly if it was a special occasion. "Yes, I am going to propose. I haven't worked out all the details yet, but I know she would love champagne and strawberries."

The staff member asked if he wanted any ideas. The guest quickly nodded and returned an hour later to learn of the Ritz's plan that would make it hard for anyone to say no. During the morning housekeeping service, a telescope was placed in the guest's room, pointed at Central Park across 59th Street. At the designated hour in the afternoon, the guest asked his girlfriend to look through the telescope, which was trained on another Ritz staff member who was across the pond holding a sign saying, "Tess, will you marry me?" And two minutes later, there was a knock on the door with champagne, strawberries, and flowers.

The plan came off without a hitch. Happily, Tess said yes.

As you hear this story, it's easy to see what it means to provide service excellence and be inspired to create remarkable experiences for your clients—a win for the client and for the firm. And a win for Wes as their leader. It was easy for him to remember his key point and be in the room while he told the story.

I heard that story once. I didn't write it down or talk about it for seven years. Last year, I was reminded of it during a conversation with another client, and I was able to retell it and get its essence across. As my wife will tell you, my memory isn't my strong suit ... What made it easy to remember was story.

To make it easy to remember and retell your message, stick it to memory with a story.

> Never underrate the power of stories. Lyndon Johnson
> got the Civil Rights Act done because of the stories he told and
> the ones [Martin Luther] King told ... Part of what I've
> always been interested in as president, and what
> I will continue to be interested in as an ex-president, is telling
> better stories about how we can work together.
>
> BARACK OBAMA

Oxy-what?

If you need more reasons to tell stories, research has shown that when we hear them, our bodies release oxytocin, also known as the trust hormone, in our brains.[9] Many people strive to be the trusted advisor. Story helps you establish and deepen trust, so you may want to use story early in your speaking to get brain chemistry to catalyze trust.

Use story to develop trust.

Top Grades for the Teacher

Research also shows that people learn better from those who tell stories.[10] The most consistently top-rated prof at my business school didn't get the grades because of his doctorate from Harvard Business School, he got them because he taught using stories drawn from consulting to Fortune 500 companies. He had the build of a point guard and eyes that seemed to suggest he already knew what you were going to say—because he probably did. He would stroll in front of the class and reference a thought he had had while driving to school in his little red sports car, apropos of nothing. Then he'd tell us how he helped a national drug store chain boost its profitability by 10 percent by advising them to expand their product assortment (sell more groceries) and luxury items (cosmetics) to draw more traffic and boost the amount spent per shopping basket. We learned more from him and his vignettes than from the other profs who'd written the textbook but not been in the aisles advising clients.

Use story to enhance learning.

Give What You Like to Receive

Many years ago, I asked my mom what gift I should give my girlfriend, now wife. She asked, "What does she give? People tend to give what they like to receive." Good advice. While I won't tell you what I gave my girlfriend, I will ask you: As an audience, would you rather hear a long recitation of points, bullet after nauseating bullet, or hear an expert speak to a few salient points that are illustrated with short vignettes? Which is more engaging, memorable, and compelling?

Based on ratings, *60 Minutes* is the most successful prime-time show in US television history. It's won an unsurpassed 160 Emmy awards. What's at the root of the show's success? The show's creator Don Hewitt said, "The formula is simple and it's reduced to four words every kid in the world knows: Tell me a story. It's that easy."[11]

Easy for Hewitt. Yet most experts are logical, left-brained thinkers who aren't natural storytellers. If you're not a gifted raconteur, that's okay. A framework and a few tips can help you stitch together a small story and help you make a bigger impact.

The Story Builder

There are many classic storytelling models, such as the quest, the hero's journey, and rags to riches. These are helpful if you are writing a screenplay or novel but have less use when speaking in most organizations. Here's a simple story-building framework to help you tell better stories in a range of situations.

THE STORY BUILDER

1 Get the listener invested	2 Spark insight and discovery	3 Deliver a payoff
Introduce a likable protagonist. + Create tension.	Provide a solution that lets people learn something or reinforces a timeless lesson.	Resolve the tension and include inspiring (or repelling) results. + Close the loop to connect the story to your broader message. Doing so ensures you have a point!

Common threads to be woven through all three parts:
- Add texture and details.
- Include emotionally charged dialogue.
- Be authentic.
- Be credible and avoid hyperbole.
- Ensure the story is consistent with your objective.

GET THE LISTENER INVESTED

What TV show foreshadowed binge-watching? The term was coined in 2003 with the increasing popularity of Netflix. Just prior to that, you may have found yourself watching a succession of episodes of 24 on DVD. It starred Kiefer Sutherland as counterterrorist agent Jack Bauer, who races against time to thwart attacks, presidential assassinations, and mass explosions—lots of tension.

Rarely had people invested so much time in such a short time frame watching a series. 24 gets you invested—at the end of each episode, you're in so much suspense you just have to keep watching to see if Bauer foils the catastrophe and resolves the tension. How can you get listeners invested in listening to you, even if you're not producing political thrillers? There are two parts:

1 **Make it personal**—First, the story needs to be about individual people (Jack Bauer and the president), not a group (the counterterrorism unit). Notice how the sports media build hype for a team contest by pitching it as a battle between two players: Tom Brady versus Nick Foles, Kawhi Leonard versus Steph Curry, Clayton Kershaw versus Tyler Glasnow. A typical sports headline to illustrate: "Megan Rapinoe vs. Lucy Bronze in a World Cup Semifinal Is a Star-Power Matchup Like No Other."[12] The media love to tease the drama out further by trying to get the players to comment on each other like boxers leading up to a title fight. It works, whipping fans into a frenzy by getting them invested in the match.

Focusing on individuals over groups has been proven to work.[13] Researcher Paul Slovic at University of Oregon has shown that people are more willing to make charitable donations to help one starving girl than that same girl and millions of others who are starving.[14]

> It's always about stories . . . Story, to be vivid,
> has to be about an individual case. And when you
> dilute it by adding cases, you dilute the emotion.
>
> DANIEL KAHNEMAN, WINNER OF THE NOBEL
> PRIZE IN ECONOMICS

2 **Insert an obstacle**—The second thing you need to do to get the listener invested is to put an obstacle between a person and their aspirations. In Slovic's study, the obstacle to the girl achieving her (implicit) aspiration of living a good life is starvation.

Let's say you have a client, Sage, who's a former surf champion living in Santa Cruz, California. She called you and said, "Hey, I've built a cult following for my sweet, hand-shaped surfboards called Ripline. Dudes from beach bums to i-bankers have been telling me for years that the Ripline gives them the sweetest ride. They hang my boards as art in their living room when they're not using them." She has lots of praise, but not a lot of cash. "I want to raise some money so I can buy machinery to scale up production and sell to a global chain. They love my boards. But I don't want to borrow money from a bank and I don't have rich friends. I want to see my fiberglass babies on the best waves around the world."

Now we have a likable protagonist—it's hard to get a listener to pull for a jerk—with tension between her global aspirations and her capital constraints. This creates anticipation and uncertainty. You want her to make it, but you aren't sure she will.

The obstacle can also come from putting your protagonist in a pickle. In the Danny Boyle film *127 Hours*, Utah adventurer Aron Ralston has got his arm stuck under a boulder in a slot canyon. If he can't free himself, he will die. What happens? You'll have to watch it to find out.

Kurt Vonnegut called this the man-in-a-hole story.[15] Maybe your client thinks one of her employees is embezzling funds and the business is hemorrhaging cash. What do you do to get her out of the hole?

Drama is anticipation coupled with uncertainty.
ATTRIBUTED TO WILLIAM ARCHER, LITERARY CRITIC

People love the drama of anticipation and uncertainty. That's why millions watch sporting events on TV as they happen, rather than stream them after the fact when there is no uncertainty—the outcome of the match has been decided. Sage needs a solution, and the listener wants to find out if she gets one.

SPARK INSIGHT AND DISCOVERY

Now you could explain what you did to help her: "I got Sage to ask her i-banker fans if they'd buy some equity in her business. I drew up a letter to explain the offer to these potential investors."

Ideally, the solution sparks insight or discovery for the listener. In this simple example, perhaps the audience is young entrepreneurs who aren't aware of capital sources other than bank debt and don't realize their customers could be their funders.

I was speaking with Jon Lax, a founding partner of the world-renowned design firm Teehan+Lax. He was standing on polished concrete in a glass-cubed boardroom when he said, "I try to build my story to an *aha* moment. I look to movies for inspiration, like the moment in *The Usual Suspects* when you realize that Verbal Kint is Keyser Söze." He smiled as his eyebrows rose. "I hope that isn't a plot spoiler!" He continued, "All the pieces that have been laid out come together."

He rolled up the sleeves on his plaid shirt, revealing forearms that would win wrestling matches. "I think about what's my *aha* moment or one insight and how can I build the narrative to get to it." To illustrate, he explained that his firm had done work for a large real estate broker, and when he went to present their initial creative, he took the client through a set of analyses and improvements before saying, "But one of the worst parts of the online experience for the online buyer is when they return to any real estate website, they have to start all over again." He pointed to an imaginary image behind him and continued, "I showed them the screen. I didn't have to use words. They could just see that our design made complete sense, and no one had thought of this before. We designed something that remembered everything you did. You didn't need to sign in. It just remembered it—it just worked the way you'd expect it." *Aha* delivered.

DELIVER A PAYOFF

A business story should usually end with a payoff that resolves the tension and includes results. In Sage's case, she raised the money from her i-banker customers and jacked up her annual sales from low six to low seven figures. As surfers would say, "That's epic, dude." Payoff indeed.

People often fail to include a result at the end of their story. Some take the result for granted: they lived the example and know how things came together—Sage got the financing and sales lift. Others don't want to seem like they are grandstanding. Notice the lead character in the story is Sage, though, not you. You are the supporting actor. Subordinating your role is important, to avoid the appearance of boasting, while subtly showing how you can help others.

> **People have forgotten how to tell a story. Stories don't have a middle or an end anymore. They usually have a beginning that never stops beginning.**
>
> STEVEN SPIELBERG

Ensure you close the loop: explain how the story connects to a broader message or audience takeaway. Now is often not the time to be implicit when you could be explicit, as in, "Remember, you don't have to take on debt to grow your company. Your best investors may be your existing customers, standing—or surfing—right in front of you." Closing the loop ensures your story has a point and the audience sees it.

When you pick the right story, it will take your listener on a little journey from, "That sounds like me..." to, "I want that too." Stories are Power Messages. You want the listener pulling for and identifying with the protagonist. If you're doing it right, the listener will want the same outcome as the protagonist.

COMMON THREADS TO ENRICH THE STORY

Here are five things to try to include in all three parts of the story.

1 **Add texture and details**—Malcolm Gladwell is at home in a library's stacks reading dusty journals, plumbing them for big ideas. His hair defies gravity and appears as though he tugs it outward during marathon research sessions. When he finds the big idea, he masterfully builds a relatable story to share it. His first five books were on the *New York Times* bestsellers list, including *Blink*, *Outliers*, and *The Tipping Point*. His TED talks have been viewed over 15 million times, and he commands tens of thousands of dollars to take the podium. His initial podcast has been so successful, he's started a production company, Pushkin Industries, to make more podcasts with other gifted storytellers.

Every time he introduces a character—even a relatively minor one—Gladwell almost always includes a one-sentence physical description of the players in his piece, to give them shape and definition in your imagination. At TED, he introduced the main character in his talk, "Choice, Happiness, and Spaghetti Sauce," this way: "Howard's about this high, and he's round, and he's in his sixties, and he has big huge glasses and thinning gray hair, and he has a kind of wonderful exuberance and vitality, and he has a parrot, and he loves the opera, and he's a great aficionado of medieval history." Gladwell also begins almost every story by specifying the date and the place.

Details make a story more believable. Research has found eyewitness testimony is more effective if it includes details relevant to the case.[16] But beware: there are diminishing returns on details, so don't overdo them.

Add texture and details to your stories. Name and briefly describe the characters. When I get my clients to do this, their faces warm and their voices animate in a way that humanizes them and makes their story more relatable and believable.

2   **Include emotionally charged dialogue**—I was on the executive floor of a mirrored glass building, sitting across from an exec in the energy business. She wore bold stripes and structured jackets and square-heeled pumps. She said, "That guy was so unbelievably arrogant that I will never hire anyone from that firm again!" He was the lead day-to-day manager of a million-dollar project delivered to her company, and this was her overriding takeaway as a client. I asked her, "Did you tell the head of the client team?"

"I would have if they were interested enough to ask. But they didn't. We spend over $10 million a year on their services, and their piece of the pie? Poof! It's gone."

Which is more interesting: stating my client has no tolerance for arrogance, or bringing this sentiment alive with dialogue? Which encourages you to get animated when you speak? The easiest way to authentically enliven your voice is to plan content that is conducive to getting animated ("Poof!") and use your hands to punctuate the point. Try it.

The Top 100 use dialogue every other minute, on average. Brian Little is one of them. He is a professor of psychology at Harvard who studies and talks about introversion and extroversion. In his talk, "Who Are You, Really? The Puzzle of Personality," he told the audience at TED that he's about as extreme an introvert as one could imagine.

He looked the professorial part: comfortable black leather shoes, a burgundy pocket square to match his wool crewneck sweater, and locks about a month past their best-before date.

He said to the gathering, "I thought I would tell you a few facts and stories, in which you may catch a glimpse of yourself." To illustrate how introverts and extroverts communicate differently, he told a story of an experience working with his extroverted colleague, Tom, who he said is as different from him as two people could be.

He explained they'd seconded a person called Michael to work on the project. When the project came to a halt, the person who'd seconded Michael asked Little and his colleague:

> "What do you make of Michael?"
>
> I said, "Well, Michael does have a tendency at times of behaving in a way that some of us might see as perhaps more assertive than is normally called for."
>
> Tom rolled his eyes and he said, "Brian, that's what I said: he's an asshole!"
>
> Now, as an introvert, I might gently allude to certain "assholic" qualities in this man's behavior, but I'm not going to lunge for the A-word. But the extrovert says, "If he walks like one, if he talks like one, I call him one." And we go past each other.

Little's talk came alive in this vibrant exchange. The dialogue animated him as he illustrated his point, and it played a key role in moving his audience to their feet.

James Veitch is on his way to the tip of the Top 100 list. His brilliant talk "This Is What Happens When You Reply to Spam Email" is entirely constructed on a dialogue-driven story. It's not the kind of talk you will likely deliver, but if you've yet to watch it, you should.

3 **Be authentic**—"I can't talk about F1. I don't watch car racing— it's not me!" Linda was pretty committed to this position. She leads a team of 6,000 professionals. People admire her, and for good reason. She combines the intensity of a professional athlete, the careful plotting of a strategist, and the charisma of a *Saturday Night Live* host. And she's authentic.

"I don't want you to talk about things that aren't you either," I replied. "What if you had an authentic reason to talk about F1?" Then she recalled that she and her daughter had visited Monte Carlo, where the Monaco Grand Prix F1 race takes place every spring. She remembered talking to others about the race and learning about the "sport"—her air quotes, not mine. Using this recollection gave her an authentic gateway to get into the story, which she used to shift her team's thinking about their approach to collaboration.

Your stories should be true to your character. As you filter potential stories, don't prematurely cast aside good stories that don't initially seem authentic to you. Sometimes you just need an authentic way to get into the story.

4   **Be credible**—I've overheard someone say to a colleague, "Oh man, I don't believe her. She exaggerates everything!" There's a line between embellishing to add color to a story and exaggeration or outright hyperbole. The latter erodes credibility. To preserve it, don't cross the line; or if you do, consider owning it: "I'm exaggerating for effect..."

Credibility is rooted in veracity. A litigator named Geoff told me, "We always advise clients before testifying, 'Be forthright in admitting your flaws.'" Our stories can be more credible if we acknowledge shortcomings within them.

5   **Be consistent with your objective**—While stories are great, we shouldn't tell them without a purpose. The story should be consistent with achieving your communication objectives. If you want your audience to become a mentor, you might want to tell a story about how another mentor made a difference in a young professional's life and how rewarding it was for both parties. Maybe the junior learned how to pick projects to gain valuable experience and the senior learned how to use some new software.

Here's how Sage's example fits into the Story Builder rubric:

1 Get the listener invested	2 Spark insight and discovery	3 Deliver a payoff
Introduce a likable protagonist. + Create tension. Sage's aspiration: scale production of her surfboards and sell them globally. Sage's challenge: she needs capital and doesn't want to go into debt, creating tension with her aspiration.	Provide a solution that lets people learn something or reinforces a timeless lesson. Sage learned about equity financing and the importance of tapping your existing network of fans for potential investors.	Resolve the tension and include inspiring (or repelling) results. + Close the loop to connect the story to your broader message. Doing so ensures you have a point! Sage raised the money and increased her sales tenfold. There are many sources of capital, including your fans.

Common threads to be woven through all three parts:
- Add texture and details. (Sage is a surf champ, she lives in Santa Cruz, and her brand is Ripline.)
- Include emotionally charged dialogue. ("I want to see my fiberglass babies on the best waves around the world" and "That's epic!")
- Be authentic. (Sage is your client and you arrange private financing, so it makes sense for you to tell the story.)
- Be credible and avoid hyperbole.
- Ensure the story is consistent with your objective. (The story reinforces the objectives to teach equity financing and networking.)

HOW MANY STORIES SHOULD YOU TELL?

As a benchmark, the Top 100 tell two stories in an eighteen-minute talk—one is a personal story, experienced first-hand by the speaker, and one is someone else's told second-hand. Chances are, you'll need at least one.

The best speakers, US president or PhD chemist, lavishly illustrate their talks with short, striking vignettes. In fact, the most potent speeches are often little more than strings of such vignettes, loosely linked by an outline and in support of just one or two big ideas.

TOM PETERS, STANFORD PHD IN BUSINESS, FORMER MCKINSEY PARTNER, BESTSELLING AUTHOR, AND SPEAKER

You may be thinking, "I don't sell surfboards. If I did, I'd have lots of stories. But I don't. I talk about dry concepts." Stay with me.

Let's say you have to talk about statistics. With apologies to statisticians, the last book in the world I would ever want to read is one about statistics. Unless it is written by Michael Lewis. He wrote one, *Moneyball: The Art of Winning an Unfair Game*. It was a bestseller and was turned into a movie starring Brad Pitt that was nominated for six Academy Awards. Pretty good for a book on stats.

In it, Lewis tells the story of Billy Beane, the general manager of the Oakland Athletics, and how he used statistics to try to beat teams such as the New York Yankees, who had more than three times Oakland's payroll. Lewis quickly has you rooting for Beane. He's highly competitive, although you learn he was humbled as a pro athlete. You see he's a good father to his daughter. There's tension between Beane's tiny payroll and his huge desire to beat the marquee teams with massive payrolls. You want Beane to win. Even if he doesn't win the World Series, it's a thrill to watch him try. Lewis uses the story of a struggling character to show the power of statistics to get an unfair advantage. Find your Billy Beane and you too can bring a dry subject to life.

WHAT ABOUT CONFIDENTIALITY?

If you are concerned about breaching client confidentiality, here are a few options: ask for permission to tell the story; anonymize the details by removing or changing the identifiers (names, industry, data); or create a hypothetical example, which we will discuss in a moment.

TYPES OF STORIES

Here are three different types of stories you may find helpful to tell in work-related situations:

1 **Hypothetical: Create the unreal to make your idea relatable**—Let's acknowledge that tax lawyers aren't typically seen as the most engaging speakers. Fortunately, there are outliers like David. A tall Southerner with a polished head where he perches his reading glasses, he is a musician who practices law in New York City. Not the prototypical tax pro. He wowed a crowd talking about—wait for it— tax compliance.

He got up in front of an audience of non-tax professionals and said, "Let me introduce you to Bubba. Now I'm from Texas, so I can use the name Bubba with pride. Bubba has been living and working in Europe for ten years. Now let's say Bubba has invested in some IBM shares, which he purchased at $10 per share and then sold for $110."

As he unfolded the story, David sketched on a whiteboard wall a series of places Bubba had lived and the investments he had made there: "Bubba had grown a taste for burgundy wine and wound up buying a villa in Beaune, France, where he lives with his bullmastiff, Butch." While there, Bubba could not resist buying a stock called Alibaba when it first came on the market at US $68.

Then he asked the audience, "What tax is Bubba obliged to pay in the United States, where he hasn't lived for two decades?"

Not surprisingly, the audience was wrong in their responses. David went on to explain why Americans have new tax obligations because of FATCA, the Foreign Account Tax Compliance Act.

One of David's partners in the audience said, "That was the most entertaining and informative tax talk I've ever heard."

It can be hard to make abstract topics interesting, but if you create a hypothetical scenario to take your audience from the general (American expat investors) to the specific (Bubba living in Beaune, investing in Alibaba), you are on your way to standing out from the crowd.

Draw your audience in from the general to the specific using hypothetical scenarios.

2 **Stealth case study: Use story to bring problem-solving to life**—The last thing we want to do is stand out unfavorably. That's what terrified Robin when he called me and said, "I've been given a grenade of a topic, and I'm going to die on stage."

Robin is a father of three who would be the first to admit he is too busy to get his curly hair under control or even clean his tortoise-rimmed glasses. He'd recently made partner in his firm and was keen to build his profile, so he asked his colleagues in marketing to help him land speaking engagements. They delivered, much to his initial horror.

I asked him to tell me more. "My topic is not only dry and boring, but it is of limited interest to the audience. I have to speak to 400 international patent attorneys in New York City on Canada's experience of changing how we protect innovations. What was it like for us to move from what is called 'first to invent' to 'first to file.'"

"That sounds tough," I said.

"Oh, I'm not done. I have the worst timeslot of the all-day conference—1:30 pm, when everyone in the room falls asleep after lunch. And to cement my demise, the most senior members of my firm will be in the audience watching me as I self-destruct."

After a few deep breaths and some laughs, he got down to work preparing. He created two hypothetical inventors who wanted to protect their work: a Canadian named Jean-Jacques Canuck and an American named Yankee Doodle. Both had invented body armor made out of pork. The Canadian had fashioned a piece of hockey equipment out of frozen bacon with the added benefit that you could thaw it, cook it, and eat it after the match. The American had developed a flak jacket made out of pork bellies. He outlined how each inventor would protect their inventions—in the United States under first to invent, in Canada under first to file—as a way of explaining the way Canada used to be, the way it and the rest of the world is now, and the way the United States may go one day.

During the coffee break that afternoon, people approached Robin and made unsolicited comments such as, "What a breath of fresh air. I learned something, and it was entertaining to boot!"

When your speaking situation is looking dire, Robin reminds us that sometimes you don't need a cape, just a little creativity in the form of a hypothetical scenario. It may not be real, but it can make a dry topic entertaining and informative.

Hypotheticals don't need to be spun into a story. They can simply stand in as a real example. The Top 100 use a non-story hypothetical scenario every three minutes.

Did Robin's speech, or even my story about Robin, read like a case study? No. But both are, hidden in the wrapper of a story.

The first part of my story outlined the situation Robin was in and created tension (topic not relevant, bad speaking slot, senior partners judging him). The solution was to use fictitious inventors to explain how different intellectual property regimes work. The result was the positive audience feedback (learned something and it was entertaining).

This case study may have taken some readers on a quick journey from, "That sounds like a situation I could be in," to, "I want those outcomes too." Power Messages elicited by a case study, hidden in a story.

If it makes sense for your objectives and the audience's needs, a case study may be a great approach to help you educate and inspire confidence in you and your ideas. Case studies don't have to sound like they're prepared for a scientific journal. Dress them up in story and you will create more sparks.

Spin hypothetical case studies into stories to make dry topics engaging.

Here's how my story about Robin's swine inventors fits into the Story Builder:

1 **Get the listener invested**	2 **Spark insight and discovery**	3 **Deliver a payoff**
Introduce a likable protagonist. + Create tension. Robin's aspiration: raise profile and do a good job speaking. Robin's challenge: topic is not relevant; bad speaking slot; senior colleagues watching in the audience.	Provide a solution that lets people learn something or reinforces a timeless lesson. Robin created two inventors and used them to explain how each would protect their intellectual property in their respective countries to explain the different approaches.	Resolve the tension and include inspiring (or repelling) results. + Close the loop to connect the story to your broader message. Doing so ensures you have a point! Robin received unsolicited, positive feedback.

Common threads to be woven through all three parts:
- Add texture and details. (Robin is father of three, tortoise-rimmed glasses; speaking to 400 patent attorneys in NYC at 1:30 pm; Jean-Jacques Canuck, Yankee Doodle, body armor made out of pork.)
- Include emotionally charged dialogue. ("I have the worst speaking slot...self-destruct." And the audience member, "What a breath of fresh air. I learned something and it was entertaining to boot!")
- Be authentic.
- Be credible and avoid hyperbole.
- Ensure the story is consistent with your objective. (The story reinforces that you can make dry topics relatable using hypothetical scenarios.)

3   **Analogy: Use a parallel story to shift perspective and generate possibility**—If you could adopt a grandfather, Benjamin Zander would be at the top of many people's wish list. His passion bursts into the room, and he seems to have a static charge in his silver hair. He's the music director of the Boston Philharmonic Orchestra and its youth orchestra

and the coauthor of *The Art of Possibility*. He's committed to helping others see and pursue brighter futures. He's a Top 100 speaker, and in 2008, he riveted the TED crowd with "The Transformative Power of Classical Music" and shared a timeless allegory:

Probably a lot of you know the story of the two salesmen who went down to Africa in the 1900s. They were sent down to find if there was any opportunity for selling shoes, and they wrote telegrams back to Manchester. And one of them wrote, "Situation hopeless. Stop. They don't wear shoes." And the other one wrote, "Glorious opportunity. They don't have any shoes yet."

Now Zander was explicit with his analogy as he connected opportunities in shoes with classical music: "There are some people who think that classical music is dying. And there are some of us who think, 'You ain't seen nothing yet.' And rather than go into statistics and trends...I thought we should do an experiment tonight. Actually, it's not really an experiment, because I know the outcome."

Zander went on to show the audience how classical music could transform them, not just in front of them, but with them. He got the room of 1,600, most of whom thought they were tone deaf, to hum the final note of a Chopin piece. They sang it in tune on the first try. He returned to another shoe story at the end to tie together his argument and leave his audience with a rekindled desire to enjoy and share classical music. Bravo Ben, yet again.

To see the power of story-as-analogy in the commercial world, let's look at professional silos.

Here's a multi-billion-dollar challenge in the professional service world: How do you get a group of siloed professionals to transform how they work together across disciplines? We see siloed service everywhere. How often have you had to coordinate the care for yourself or a loved one in a hospital? Many patients struggle to figure out whose expertise they should seek and how to get the right information shared.

At the world-renowned Mayo Clinic, they go about things differently: they have a team-based approach. They assemble a team to review each patient's needs, allowing them to provide better, more thoughtful and coordinated care.

For decades consultants, accountants, and advisors have all focused on providing their respective capabilities to clients, not coordinating them. But few are delivering a rich, seamless service. The world needs less silo and more Mayo.

So how do you get people to shift their siloed mindset? Well, if you're Miyo—not Mayo—the head of talent for a 10,000-person-plus firm, you talk about restaurants. Not just any, but The NoMad and Eleven Madison Park.

Miyo is an exec whose bright floral-print jackets and optimistic charge are befitting someone who tops lists of the most powerful. She stood up on a T-shaped stage and asked 2,000 of her colleagues, "How would you transform fine dining? If you are like most, your thinking would follow one of two lines: focus on the experience in the dining room or focus on the food created in the kitchen." She explained that historically, restaurants have been led by one or the other, not both. "Until David Humm partnered with Will Guidara. They just achieved the number one spot on the World's 50 Best Restaurant list, to add to their constellation of Michelin stars," she said.

Then Miyo filled in the backstory of their novel approach and how it creates standout experiences. Humm is a chef who worked in high-end, Michelin-ranked restaurants in Europe such as Gasthaus zum Gupf, located near the medieval university town of St. Gallen in the Swiss Alps. When he was looking at buying Eleven Madison Park, he realized that he needed a *partner*—not an employee—to run the dining room. The stress and perfectionism in these haute kitchens are so high some chefs commit suicide if they lose a Michelin star. Humm spent six years working sixteen-hour days in an haute kitchen, and not once did he enter the dining room. He had no idea what happened to his food after it was passed from the kitchen to the dining room.

Unusually for a chef, Humm believes that our best food memories are based on being with people we love in a nice environment eating good food. But the food alone doesn't create the memory. Everything has to work together. So he partnered with Will Guidara, who grew up in fine dining and has a passion for service. This partnership created magic. Drawing from what she learned about them from a *Vanity Fair* interview with the pair, Miyo explained that they believe their restaurants are a place for their diners to connect with each other, and they design the experience to encourage these connections. "They put the partially cut bread in the center of the table, so everyone has to reach in and break it," Miyo said, her arm reaching forward to the middle of an imaginary table. "Sometimes they incorporate a game, such as Name that Milk. They bring four bars of chocolate, each made with different milk: cow, goat, sheep, and buffalo. People have to guess what milk is in each bar, which creates an intimate experience and a bond around the table."[17]

Makes you want to be at that table, doesn't it? People's cravings go beyond the plate—we crave a genuine human connection, and Humm and Guidara provide it. They recognize that some of this magic can be designed in advance, and yet some of the most powerful experiences are created when they go off script. Miyo shared that they have a "Dreamweaver" on staff whose sole job is to create magical moments. She brought this to life:

> Guidara says, "We want our restaurants to be a bit of magic in a world that increasingly needs some more magic." He was near a family who was visiting from Europe and one of them said, 'Man, this has been the best trip ever to New York. We've eaten at so many amazing restaurants. The only thing we missed was a New York City street hot dog.'"

Modeling what it means to be a Dreamweaver, Guidara went to his partner, Miyo explained, and said, "Chef, okay, I know you've spent the last twenty years perfecting your cuisine. I kind of want to go out to the sidewalk and buy a street hot dog and serve it to them as their next course."

Miyo reinforced they were only able to do this because the partners had a mutual trust. Humm made it beautiful, adding some of his sauerkraut and relish before they served it. After all the work that was done to make it one of the best meals of the diners' lives, the hot dog was the highlight. "Guidara said, 'It's the moments when you improvise that make it memorable. So you train your staff to listen for those moments.'"

At this point, Miyo's audience was drawn in, listening carefully. Understandably, some of them may have been wondering what all this talk of name-that-chocolate and street-dogs-with-sauerkraut has to do with their advisory services. Well, Miyo served up her answer: "We need to train our staff to listen and to improvise. And we need to recognize that when we only bring one silo of service to the market, we are limiting the experience." She paused before adding, "It's the dining room hospitality and the kitchen working together and trusting each other that will help us be unmatched in serving our clients."

By the time Miyo got off stage, she received a number of requests from her partners to re-deliver her talk in other forums. Her colleagues wrote about how her message had resonated and about their plans to talk to their teams about Dreamweavers the next day. This was a room full of left-brained, data-driven professionals who responded to story.

Good stories always beat good spreadsheets.

CHRIS SACCA, ANGEL INVESTOR

Use story as an analogy to explain strategy and align the iron filings.

Analogy and Metaphor

Stories can be analogies, but analogies don't have to be in stories, of course. Metaphors and their comparative cousins analogy and simile are not novel. From Churchill's "iron curtain" to Martin Luther King Jr.'s "I've been to the mountaintop . . . And I've seen the promised land," the greatest speeches in history are loaded with metaphor. But metaphors are often missing in most people's remarks—a missed opportunity to be clear and memorable.

Symphonic Stabbings and Bloody Conductors

Imagine you are standing at the podium facing away from the audience and toward a hundred members of one of the world's great orchestras. How would you tell these professionals to play a piece with more intensity?

If you are Gustavo Dudamel, Venezuelan-born conductor and musical director of the Los Angeles Philharmonic, you would liken the intensity to violently stabbing somebody with a knife. "It's good, this," as he makes a stabbing motion with his baton, "but the blood is not coming." He adds, "The blood needs to be in your face," as he shoots his hands up to depict the blood spraying on his face.[18]

He stands before the orchestra with a taut black tee on his athletic build. Conductors on premiere stages don't normally have builds you'd like to see in tight clothes (he became a conductor upon realizing his arm was too short to play the trombone). As he gets the orchestra to play again, he leads them with bone-breaking baton movements that reverberate through the ringlets of his hair and grunts you'd expect to hear on a tennis court, not a concert stage.

They stop. "Now we have blood! A lot."

Dudamel is so talented that by twenty-six, he'd already conducted at La Scala in Milan, the Vienna Philharmonic at the Lucerne Festival, and the Stuttgart Radio Symphony Orchestra at the Vatican. The LA Philharmonic's conductor is typically someone of Benjamin Zander's vintage, not a young Spanish-speaking spark plug. Dudamel was twenty-seven when he was offered the job.

When you read his bio, you see he has deep classical training. But when you see him communicate, you understand how he gets a band of pros to play in a way that audiences love. As we've seen, metaphor is one of his key tools.

I was so taken seeing his performance on TV that I researched his tour dates and bought my first-ever ticket to the Toronto Symphony Orchestra—to watch him conduct, rather than to listen to the music. He was mesmerizing. Classical music never sounded so good.

Metaphors are powerful, particularly when speaking about abstract things like playing with intensity, in Dudamel's case. Top 100 speakers use one of them every three minutes. Few of my clients use any. When you do, they can vault you to bigger stages.

Why do they work so well? There is a range of reasons, so let's dive in.

JELLY DONUTS AND YOUR DIAGNOSIS

"You know that 'doctor' in Latin is *docēre*, which means to teach. I take this part of my job seriously—not just with med students, but patients as well." This was Dr. Doug Richards's response when I thanked him for always explaining things to me in a way that's clear and not condescending.

Richards has been the clinical director at University of Toronto's David L. MacIntosh Sport Medicine Clinic since 1989. He always seems to wear cotton that's never found the underside of an iron. His clothes may not have been pressed, but his communication is always impressive.

Most of us at some point will be on the receiving end of an important diagnosis from a doctor. If there's ever a time we want to clearly understand an expert, it's when they are telling us what's happening in our bodies. Enter comparative devices.

Let's say you just bought a mid-century modern credenza to hold your TV and you slipped while lifting it. You've thrown out your back and, it turns out, you have a herniated disk. Dr. Richards might explain that a disk is a cushion between two vertebrae in your spine. It has an outer layer that is tougher and an inner layer that is softer, like a miniature jelly donut. In your case, the outer layer is cracked, and some jelly is protruding and pushing on the nerve—a herniated disk.

Analogy and metaphor are one of the most efficient ways to bridge a technical divide, as they tap into a parallel frame of reference the listener understands. And maybe we get a mood boost when hearing people mention donuts during diagnosis.

Use analogy and metaphor to bridge a technical divide.

BUFFETT ON GETTING BUFFETED

If you pay passing attention to the stock market, you will see that certain stocks are often popular—and overpriced—in the short term. We've seen this with areas such as social media, cannabis, or office- or ride-sharing securities. How would you explain how stock prices behave in the short term versus the long term?

"In the short run, the market is a voting machine... but in the long run, the market is a weighing machine."[19] This is an explanation used by Warren Buffett. While many might explain volatility using formulas with Greek letters and talk of deviation from the mean, Buffett's explanation is clear and brings calm to those getting buffeted by short-term volatility. (He could add the Greek-lettered explanation for those with more background knowledge—something you're prompted to think about when you Shrink the Wall.)

Warren Buffett is widely considered the world's greatest investor. He has a gift for explaining complex ideas with clarity and color. When investors like Buffett are starting out, they need capital to allocate. How do they get it? By communicating with clarity in a way that engenders confidence.

"Good portfolio managers are a dime a dozen. Good portfolio managers who can sell are worth millions," said Bill Holland, chairman of CI Financial, one of the largest investment companies in Canada. In Buffett's case, he's worth billions. He's a rare technician who explains complex concepts clearly. He's built a massive flywheel whose momentum is generated by his investing performance *and* his ability to convey ides clearly—and he uses comparative devices masterfully to do so.

Use analogy and metaphor to make your stock rise.

WIFFLE BALL OR LIVE FIRE

Whether you are on stage or on a call, you can use metaphor to create levity and humor. Jerry Seinfeld does a bit about how those who are married cannot relate to the unmarried. "I can't hang out with single guys. You don't have a wife; we have nothing to talk about. You have a girlfriend? That's Wiffle ball, my friend. You're playing paintball war; I'm in Afghanistan with real, loaded weapons."[20]

Use comparative devices to add personality and humor.

I think you are out of your mind if you keep taking jobs that you don't like because you think it will look good on your résumé... Isn't that a little like saving up sex for your old age? There comes a time when you ought to start doing what you want.

WARREN BUFFETT

LESSONS FROM A DECORATED LEADER

After Colin Powell retired from his political and military career, where he served as Secretary of State, Chairman of the Joint Chiefs of Staff, and National Security Advisor, he wrote two memoirs and established a career as a speaker. In his talk on leadership, he cautioned about being influenced by others, saying, "Don't be buffaloed by experts and elites. Experts often possess more data than judgment. Elites can become so inbred that they produce hemophiliacs who bleed to death as soon as they are nicked by the real world."[21] How many metaphors do you count in that passage?

Use metaphor to make your message vivid.

HEAD, TAIL, OR TORSO?

Let's play word association. What's the first word that comes into your head when you think of "vice president of design at a tech firm"? If that leader is Jon Lax, one word you'd say is strategist. As I mentioned earlier, Lax was one of the founding partners at the design firm Teehan+Lax. In January 2015, they were acquired by a Silicon Valley firm whose platform is used by the equivalent of one-third of the world's population every month.

When a big chunk of the world uses your product, how do you decide what you should build and for whom? Lax works to answer this question. At one time, he wrote a note suggesting where his organization should prioritize their attention. In it he used the head, torso, and tail of a power law curve to define three major market segments.

Companies in the head are large and sophisticated, those in the torso are mid-sized, and the tail holds small mom-and-pop shops. Lax explained the needs of each group and the opportunities to build products for them and in what order. His note was circulated among the executive ranks, and pretty soon he was on stage in front of a global gathering of one of their biggest divisions explaining the head, torso, and tail. People adopted and used this anatomical shorthand.

Use analogy to crystalize thinking, shape strategy, and increase your profile.

BEFORE YOU GO TO MARKET, GET A HOLD OF YOUR METAPHOR

"I don't tell you how to write your stories. So don't tell me how to market my company. I know marketing," shot Marc Benioff to a writer who offered marketing advice to the founder of Salesforce.com.[22]

He's grown Salesforce from launch in 1999 to a market value of over US $160 billion in twenty years. So yes, he knows how to market. In the early days, he would say Salesforce was Amazon meets Siebel Systems. Siebel was a traditional software giant. "Our story was that the big evil software companies were extorting millions from customers. And the internet was coming to save these customers." Benioff related his offering to what was already familiar.

When asked about the most common marketing mistake entrepreneurs make, he said, "Before talking to the media, get a hold of your metaphor. This isn't a sound bite. It's a metaphor that is easy to understand... Journalists will use your metaphor in their story because they can't come up with one on their own. It is a hard, not trivial, thing to do. And I spend hours and hours on this, because I think it is so crucial to getting the message out."

Get the right message out through metaphor.

Trying to campaign on complex policy issues is like trying to sell steamed Brussels sprouts in a candy store.

TERRY O'REILLY, FOUNDER OF PIRATE RADIO AND
PRODUCER OF *UNDER THE INFLUENCE*

Getting a hold of your metaphor is important when talking to any audience. As Benioff notes, it's hard to come up with them, so let's examine how you can do so.

How Do You Come Up With Them?

Two things typically stand in the way of most people using analogy and metaphor. A left-brained bias can make it tough. I hear many say, "I'm just not good at it." Others feel the need to have the perfect comparator, or they won't use one.

Here's a simple question that helps create possibilities: Where else in your life do you see something that looks like the concept you want to talk about? Think through various aspects of your life to find similarities.

One of my clients was speaking to 800 partners of the organization he leads. They had experienced considerable growth, and he was worried many of his partners would think they had maximized their revenue and would become complacent. He was convinced there was upside to be captured in the year ahead. This situation reminded him of an experience he had had cycling in the Alps. He'd spent hours climbing a mountain, wending his way up the switchbacks. On numerous occasions, he thought he'd made the summit, only to discover when he rounded the bend there was still more to climb. These were false summits. They looked like the top, but they weren't.

He drew a parallel to their business. They'd worked, climbed, and achieved. But these achievements were interim, false summits, and they were on their way to even greater heights. It was evocative, helped framed their position, and humanized him—he connected a passion from his personal life to their future.

Ask: Where else in life do I see something that looks like my central idea?

PERSONALITY AND THE UNEXPECTED PLATFORM

The more pressure you are under when you need to speak, the less likely it is that your personality will show up. When you mine your personal life for analogies and metaphors, more of your personality shows up, which will strengthen your connection with the audience and the impression you make on them. Vijaye's certainly did.

Vijaye is one of my tech clients in Seattle who was speaking to more than a thousand of his colleagues. "This is cricket," he began. "It's a sport that kinda looks like baseball, but it isn't. I grew up playing this sport, watching it. And when I say watching, I mean watching and watching and watching—sometimes cricket matches take five days to finish."

He showed a picture of Melbourne's cricket stadium, which seats 100,000 fans who come to watch twenty-two players play. He described the vibrant ecosystem that is the stadium: vendors sell food, drinks, and memorabilia to fans; fans connect with the players through their cheers; GMs sit down to recruit and trade talent. He explained that the stadium is a platform for all these connections, just like the online platform his team was building to help others make meaningful connections and transact. The cricket stadium allowed the audience to learn about platforms, about their organization's strategy, and, importantly, about Vijaye as a leader and as a person.

Mine your passions for comparisons.

UNDER PRESSURE

Tapping your personal life in a way that is relevant can be a compelling and humanizing way to differentiate why you do what you do.

"My mom gave me my first watch when I was about ten," began a young professional with limited direct work experience and loads of passion. "A few days later, I took the watch apart. It was in pieces in my drawer when my mom asked, 'Where's your new watch? Why don't you show it to your cousin when she comes over in a half an hour?'"

The speaker moved a hand up to her collar and said, "I could feel the heat rising on my neck and the sweat beading on my brow. I couldn't tell her I'd ruined my new watch, so I scrambled back to my room and worked with a newfound focus to reassemble it." She paused, smiled, dropped her volume, and said, "In the twenty-ninth minute, I succeeded." The audience started to smile too. "In that moment, I became addicted to the rush of solving problems under time pressure. That's what I love about my work now." Now the listeners were nodding their heads. "I help failing companies turn their business around before they become insolvent, and I love it. Now, I try not to create my own problems, I just fix other people's broken watches."

See if you can you talk about a time in your life you learned something that informed your path to your current position. This might make for a more interesting and memorable way to introduce yourself, what you do, or what you want to talk about.

Plumb personal struggles, discoveries, and epiphanies.

WHERE ELSE IN SOMEONE ELSE'S LIFE...?

Drawing analogy and metaphor from you own life is ideal because you can speak to the comparison with comfort. If you're not having luck finding a metaphor through your own life experience, expand the circle of thought. Ask, where in your audience's life is there something that looks similar to the idea you're speaking about?

I heard a speaker waxing on about the importance of, well, wax. He asked, "What is a country that dominates cross-country skiing?" No one knew. This was more of a rugby and summer sport crowd. He answered, "Norway. Norway has owned the cross-country podium for decades. Their prowess is part heritage, part Viking physiology, and part wax." A few seconds into his treatise on wax chemistry, he could see he was losing his audience. "Do any of you cycle?" When they nodded they did, he said, "Trying to cross-country ski with the wrong kind of wax is like trying to ride a bike without air in the tires. So Norway brought not one but thirty wax technicians to the last Olympics, because it's that important." You could see they instantly got it.

Talk to a friend or colleague or even an audience member to brainstorm where else in someone else's life do they see something like what you are talking about. They may have great ideas, or a different perspective, or even a bad idea that will spark a good one for you.

You could also ask how someone with a very different perspective would explain the concept: a scientist, an artist, an athlete, a film director. Your iron curtain may be just around the corner.

Explore diverse and disparate angles with others.

LOWER THE BAR

I often ask my clients how they would explain their idea to a very smart high school student. Someone with intellect, but no context. Your answer to this question is likely to include analogy or metaphor. Sometimes an imperfect comparison is more memorable than a perfect one.

It's okay to acknowledge the imperfection, as in, "It reminds me a bit of..." or, "While it's not exactly the same, I liken it to..." As you lower the bar from finding the perfect fit, you'll likely raise the quality of your communication.

Create possibility by embracing imperfection.

Quotations

The inclusion of quotations is a time-honored tactic used by seasoned speakers. But many people don't use formal and informal quotes as often as they could. Chances are, you are one of them.

Adding Authoritative Heft

Actress Jane Fonda gave a TED address early in her eighth decade. She encouraged her audience to shift their mindset toward "Life's Third Act" by referring to this passage from Holocaust survivor Viktor Frankl's classic book *Man's Search for Meaning*: "Everything can be taken from a man but one thing: the last of the human freedoms—to choose one's attitude in any given set of circumstances." She expanded on the authoritative reference by saying, "This is what determines the quality of the life we've lived—not whether we've been rich or poor, famous or unknown, healthy or suffering. What determines our quality of life is how we relate to these realities, what kind of meaning we assign them, what kind of attitude we cling to about them, what state of mind we allow them to trigger."

You can use quotes to bring to life various client needs and customer expectations. One of my clients once recalled how a client had told her, "We don't appreciate getting billed for a $1 bag of Cheetos after a $50,000 engagement." Not Shakespearean, but a cringe-worthy way to drive home the need to review bills from a client's perspective.

Use the authority of others to reinforce your point and add a fulcrum to move your audience.

Inspiration Cocktail

These seven words were stenciled across a ten-foot office wall in a typical tinted-glass-walled office building by an airport: "I didn't come here to be average." The people inside were anything but average. They were some of the best marketers I've met in over twenty-five years—and I say that as a former brand manager for Heinz. The quote worked for them. Why?

On its own, it's bland. But what happens when the quote is attributed to Michael Jordan? The NBA's website says, "By acclamation, Michael Jordan is the greatest player of all time."[23] With Jordan's attribution, "I didn't come here to be average" carries more weight and inspiration.

While my client's core business is marketing, their main delivery mechanism is people. They know how to lead people, and using quotes from credible giants is part of their playbook.

Even professional NBA players need inspiration. The San Antonio Spurs, with the highest winning percentage among active NBA teams, has these words from Jacob Riis hanging on the wall of their locker room: "When nothing seems to help, I go and look at a stonecutter hammering away at his rock, perhaps a hundred times without as much as a crack showing in it. Yet at the hundred and first blow it will split in two, and I know it was not that last blow that did it, but all that had gone before."[24]

Propel your audience using the above-average words of others.

Outsourcing Eloquence

Nathalie took the stage in a Montreal ballroom, where she was speaking to 400 people, all leaders in her team of thousands across the country. She has the physique of a runner and wears her hair clipped in an elegant swirl rising above her head. She would prefer to speak French but most members of her team don't, so she spoke to them in English. Nathalie sets high standards for everything, including language, and gets frustrated that she can't speak eloquently in a second language.

When she was trying to convey the importance of commitment, she reached for the words of Scottish mountaineer William H. Murray: "Until one is committed, there is hesitancy, the chance to draw back, always ineffectiveness... The moment one definitely commits oneself, then Providence moves too. All sorts of things occur to help one that would never otherwise have occurred."

Then she talked about how commitment was the theme for the day, how it represents who she is, her commitment to her team, and what's required for them to achieve their future aspirations. The balance of her remarks explored how commitment threaded through four key dimensions of their business.

Whatever your mother tongue, few could convey the power of commitment as Murray did.

If you find a beautiful expression that aligns with your idea, use it.

The Tonic of Laughter

On October 27, 1940, Charlie Chaplin was quoted in the *New York Times* as saying, "Laughter is the tonic, the relief, the surcease from pain."[25] While I hope your audiences aren't in pain, they may find relief in some levity—and quotes can be a great source of it. If you were advising an audience about avoiding getting drawn into debates with naysayers, you could cite Scott Adams: "If you spend all your time arguing with people who are nuts, you'll be exhausted and the nuts will still be nuts."[26]

Add some tonic with a quote.

Quotes at the Ready

You will find it handy to have a few short quotes in your head that you can deploy on short notice. On more than one occasion, I've pulled this out of my back pocket to capture an audience's attention before setting up the need to get started doing something: "The best time to plant a tree was twenty years ago. The second-best time is now." It's a Chinese proverb and a good one to have planted in your memory.

Keep a few quotes handy in your back pocket.

Mining Wisdom

It's never been easier to find the right quote. Go to your favorite search engine and type your core idea in a word or phrase plus the word "quote"—for example, "persistence quote"—and let the internet work its magic. Then filter by finding words that fit your world view and will have the most impact based on the quote itself and the attribution. I just searched "innovation quote," and this caught my eye:

> We spend a lot of time designing the bridge, but not enough time thinking about the people who are crossing it.[27]
>
> DR. PRABHJOT SINGH, DIRECTOR OF
> SYSTEMS DESIGN AT THE EARTH INSTITUTE

It underscores the central tenet of empathy in innovation with a concrete example that also serves as a vivid metaphor. It's fresh, not hackneyed, and it comes from a credible source.

Some people collect wine, others baseball cards. I collect quotes. When you find ones you like, stash them away for later. I just put Singh's words in my shoebox.

The Top 100 use one every ten minutes on average. Don't use many more; if you do, the listener will be left with a duffel bag of phrases and no sense for who *you* are and what *you* think.

If you do use them, try to verify they're accurate. Wikiquote and Quote Investigator are good places to start.

Testimony

Conviction Alone Isn't Compelling

I used to work with someone who would state things with conviction, but his points were rarely compelling because they were empty claims. An empty claim is an assertion stated with confidence but lacking persuasiveness: "We are responsive to client needs." A first-person assertion becomes compelling when you shift it to third-party testimony from a credible source: "The head of M&A at [insert global brand] says we're the most responsive firm he's used in ten years."

Avoid making empty claims.

The Best Gift for My Brother-in-Law

"Have you ever wondered who stays up late and buys things from infomercials?" asked Greg, who was standing in front of his colleagues in a colorless meeting room in a public sector office. He raised his right hand and said, "I do! And today I want to talk to you about the best thing I have purchased in ten years of TV shopping during bouts of insomnia." He tilted forward and whispered loud enough for everyone to hear, "A vacuum sealer to preserve food called Tilia Foodsaver."

I bought one. On the strength of Greg's talk, I made my first infomercial-inspired purchase and gave the sealer to my brother-in-law, Dave, for Christmas. Dave's passions include eating great food and getting a great deal. He loves grocery shopping at Costco. The Foodsaver allows him to buy a huge piece of beef, cut it into steaks, and vacuum seal them. He throws them in the freezer and swears they are just as fresh when he cooks them months later as they were the day that he bought them. He gets as excited talking about the sealer as he does when the Raptors win.

The Foodsaver infomercial is loaded with testimony, but I didn't need to see it. Greg's endorsement was good enough for me. Research shows we place a lot of trust in the recommendations of friends and family.[28] Word-of-mouth marketing is playing a greater role in how we make decisions at the same time that trust in brands is declining. Why does it work so well? It's a shortcut that allows us to cut through piles of options and focus on the right answer because we know and trust the reviewer.

Testimony is the use of third-party comments to add credibility, persuasion, and authority. Sure, it includes formal quotations that you may publish on your website or include in your biography and proposals, but it goes beyond that. We can all benefit from using testimony more frequently and broadly in our communication.

Think about the last time that you had to choose a product, service, or experience that was really important to you—a cybersecurity expert to protect your organization's data, an expensive piece of photography equipment, a specialist to repair your cello, or a park to take your kids to on a canoe trip. How did you go about finding the right product, person, or place?

Make it easy for your listeners to trust your ideas and capabilities by including some third-party validation in your remarks.

How can you use testimony if you are not hawking wares in the wee hours of the morning?

Don't Take My Word for It

When you need to make a really important point—and really need your audience to believe it—prompt yourself by saying, "Don't take my word for it, look at what [authority X] has to say…" Find and reference the X in your remarks. You don't need to say the phrase, "Don't take my word for it" to your audience; it's just a prompt to help you come up with testimony.

Top 100 speaker Susan Cain gave a terrific TED talk on "The Power of Introverts." She explained that introverts often get overlooked for leadership positions, yet introverted leaders often deliver better outcomes than extroverts. If she were to have stopped there, she would've made an unsubstantiated claim.

You don't need to take her word for it, though; she continued, "Adam Grant at the Wharton School has found that introverted leaders often deliver better outcomes than extroverts do, because when they are managing proactive employees they're much more likely to let those employees run with their ideas, whereas an extrovert can, quite unwittingly, get so excited about things that they're putting their own stamp on things, and other people's ideas might not as easily then bubble up to the surface."

Try to finish the phrase, "Don't take my word for it…" and find compelling testimony.

Impressive Affiliations

Taylor Wilson looks like the kind of teenager that would be pushed around in high school were it not for his ability to give everyone the right answers to their science homework. At age seventeen, he told an audience he had built a nuclear fusion reactor in his garage at age fourteen! Not the kind of claim you hear every day, and one that begs credulity. (I was still figuring out how to make my bed at fourteen.)

Early in his three-minute TED talk on his work, "Yup, I Built a Nuclear Fusion Reactor," Wilson mentioned that his reactor now lives in the physics department at the University of Nevada, Reno. Wearing jeans, shirt, tie, and a vest from a three-piece suit, he rattled off further accomplishments, including winning the Intel International Science and Engineering Fair; developing a Homeland Security detector that sells for hundreds of dollars that improved upon and replaced existing detectors that cost hundreds of thousands; and visiting CERN in Geneva, Switzerland, the preeminent particle physics lab in the world. When he showed the audience a photo of himself showing President Obama his Homeland Security research, the crowd applauded for seven seconds.

In three minutes, how do we know if any of his creations work? We don't, but we're confident Wilson is more than a teenager with an affinity for science—we believe he's a bona fide nuclear physicist on the strength of the testimony of his impressive affiliations. Take them away, and he'd lose believability and his well-earned standing ovation.

The most accomplished communicators in the world use testimony. The Top 100 use a form of testimony every seventeen minutes. There's a good chance you can use it more than you do so people can buy into your reactor-building assertions without you having to split an atom in front of them.

Cite your CERN to support incredible claims.

Data

Drowning in Data

Too often people over-rely on data. They bandy about numbers indiscriminately, and the audience doesn't know what to do with them. I learned this early in my career when I was on the receiving end of presentations from Nielsen, the global market research firm that measures everything from what we watch on TV to what type of toothpaste we buy. They would come into our windowless boardroom at Heinz, turn on the overhead projector, and place a seemingly endless series of acetates on it. The sheets were packed with data—so much data that it often appeared as though Nielsen was paid by the number of numbers they presented.

What these data-driven sessions had in volume, they lacked in value. "What the heck am I supposed to do with all that?" was a standard complaint from my colleagues as we emerged from the dark room before we would begin analyzing the data—something we were paying them to do. Had they simply asked themselves, "So what?" they would have been able to move ninety slides to the appendix and focus our attention on a helpful handful of insights. But they didn't.

Don't drown your audience in data. Save them in advance by asking, "So what?"

Data and the Dead Winner

On a spring day in 2019, Tye walked on stage at Koerner Hall in Toronto under a vaulted ceiling of wooden ribbons, which creates pristine acoustics for hosting the world's best musicians. Tye wasn't there to play, but to speak, which he does with calm certainty marked with periodic spikes of intensity. The 1,100-seat auditorium was filled with people who had invested in a fund he and his partners had launched a decade prior and have since grown to over $30 billion.

He wanted to encourage investors to stick with their investments for the long haul—for their own good. "I read that Fidelity Investments did an internal study to determine which of their clients had the top-performing accounts over a ten-year period. Guess who came out on top? Dead people—the accounts belonging to the deceased. The second strongest cohort? Portfolios that people had forgotten about. Individual investors consistently underperform because they manage their portfolios too actively and buy and sell too frequently."[29]

Lesson learned: if you want to boost your investment returns, buy and hold and hold and hold, as though you were dead. Numerous studies reinforce the benefits of buying and holding, but the Fidelity analysis is indelible: two surprising data points, presented without needing specific numbers. Those like me who have held (and held) his fund have enjoyed returns that have consistently outpaced their MSCI index.

Tye is as adept at managing money as he is at communicating about investments. Unlike so many, he knows how to use data when speaking. If you don't want to deluge your audience with data, how do you select the right points?

First determine the story you want to tell, then find the right data to tell it.

From the Cockpit to the OR

When it comes to medicine, it's easy to complain about wait times and debate the role of government and insurance. But how would you actually go about improving the delivery of medicine to patients? This is a problem that Atul Gawande's been working on for years. Fortunately for us all, he's been making progress in answering the question, and his work is saving lives.

Gawande is a Harvard-trained surgeon, writer, and public health researcher. "There was a study where they looked at how many clinicians it took to take care of you if you came into a hospital, as it changed over time," he explained. "In 1970, it took just over two full-time equivalents of clinicians... By the end of the twentieth century, it had become more than fifteen clinicians for the same typical hospital patient—specialists, physical therapists, the nurses."

Gawande is tall, and his jeans bowed slightly below the pink dress shirt and blue blazer he fashioned on TED's red carpet, where he explained in "How Do We Heal Medicine?" that this rise in specialization has created a structure of siloed care, where specialists don't collaborate enough. "We have trained, hired, and rewarded people to be cowboys. But it's pit crews that we need, pit crews for patients."

Those are vivid metaphors—gold star for Gawande—and bold claims, which he substantiates with data. "Sixty percent of our asthma [and] stroke patients receive incomplete or inappropriate care." As he continues to outline the pervasiveness of the problem, you can't help but think about those you know who suffer from those conditions. "Two million people come into hospitals and pick up an infection they didn't have because someone failed to follow the basic practices of hygiene."

To find a solution, he looked to other high-risk sectors where specialists are well trained: sky-scraper construction and aviation. They used one thing that surgeons didn't: checklists.

For example, pilots have a pre-flight checklist they routinely follow. Could this simple tool help specialized surgeons get better?

Gawande's team created a two-minute, nineteen-point checklist that included simple things like making sure the antibiotic is given at the right time and unexpected things like ensuring everyone in the OR introduces themselves before every surgery, since often many in the room are coming together for the first time. They tested the checklist in eight ORs around the world. What happened? The complication rate fell by 35 percent and the death rate dropped by 47 percent.

Imagine you're an accomplished surgeon and you're being asked to use a checklist, but you're not given the data. Would you change? Once you have the data, how could you not? Gawande received a standing ovation. Next time you go into the OR, ask the surgeon if they will follow Gawande's checklist. It may be just the thing to encourage specialists to work more seamlessly and get you better.

To encourage cowboys to come together as pit crews, turbocharge your case with the right data.

What Do You Take to the Bank?

If you were making $125,000 per year, would you rather have a 12 percent raise or $15,000? Close your eyes for two seconds and commit to a choice. Turns out it's the same thing. But you had to do some math because the 12 percent is abstract. When you're the speaker, do the math for your audience. As I was told early in my career, you take dollars to the bank, not percent. Translate the percentage to the number of units, such as people or dollars, and you'll be on your way to getting a raise.

It would have been helpful if Gawande had translated the 47 percent reduction in death rate to average number of lives saved in a typical hospital that does, say, 10,000 operations a year.

Do the math for your audience.

Comparison Creates a Story

Let's look at a stat from the world of finance. Warren Buffett was worth $73.5 billion as of September 2020.[30] Yes, that's a lot of money. But *so what?* Well, he's worth as much as more than 100,000 average Americans.[31] That's equivalent to the combined worth of everyone who lives in South Bend, Indiana.

It's hard to wrap one's head around just how big a billion is. There's a fun Reddit post that explains that 1 million seconds is 11.5 days. One billion seconds is 31.7 years![32] And 73.5 billion seconds, to put Buffett's worth into context, is 2,330 years!

Michael Lewis wanted to show that the Oakland A's had come up with a more effective way to field a winning team. Lewis compared the payrolls of the A's and Yankees and determined the A's paid $260,000 per win compared to the Yankees' $1.4 million.[33] That's a David versus Goliath bestselling story, not a spreadsheet.

Turn a stat into a story by providing a comparison.

Shredding Motivation

How important is meaning in work? To understand more about this question, psychologist and behavioral economist Dan Ariely gave participants in three groups a sheet with typed letters on it. He asked them to circle all the doubled letters and return the sheet.

Ariely's early work was inspired by his experience recovering from an accident he had growing up in Israel. While preparing for a traditional nighttime ceremony, he was mixing materials that exploded and burned 70 percent of his body.[34] This experience prompted him to do research on how to deliver better care when the treatments are painful, and behavioral science more broadly.

In the circle-the-double-letters experiment, participants were paid $3 for the first sheet and then asked if they would like to do another page, but for $2.85. People were repeatedly offered another sheet, but for $0.15 less than the prior one. How many tasks would people do in groups with these conditions?

"The Acknowledged Condition"—People wrote their names on the sheet, found the letter pairs, and handed in their work. The experimenter would look at the page, say, "Uh-huh," and put it in a pile on their desk.

"The Ignored Condition"—People did not write their names on the sheet. The experimenter did not look at it and simply put it on the pile of pages.

"The Shredder Condition"—The experimenter didn't look at the work and put it directly in a shredder.

How long did people work in each of the three conditions? Not surprisingly, the Acknowledged Condition worked the longest, all the way down to getting paid only $0.15 per page. In the Shredder Condition, they worked until they were paid $0.30.

"What about the Ignored Condition? Would it be more like the Acknowledged or more like the Shredder, or somewhere in the middle?" Ariely asked the audience during his TED talk, "What Makes Us Feel Good about Our Work?" The answer is surprising. "Ignoring the performance of people is almost as bad as shredding their effort in front of their eyes."

Imagine trying to make that argument without the data. During his talk, he complemented this data with a real-world story of a big software company in Seattle. Engineers there had been working on a project for two years when the CEO called a meeting with them and told them their project was canceled.

Ariely asked the engineers how this affected them. Did they show up later than before? Yes. Did they go home earlier? You bet.

Had the CEO simply looked at their work and said, "Uh-huh," they—and he—would have been better off. Better yet, the engineers said he could have asked them to summarize and share their lessons learned and recommend how some of their work could have been used by other groups in the company. The CEO ignored the lesson that meaning matters. He shredded their motivation.

Top 100 speakers use data about once every two minutes, and you can see why. Data is a powerful tool to help you communicate.

Complement the data with a story and you're on your way to motivating people.

The Communication Trifecta

In January 1990, Jeff lived on the second floor of O'Neill residence at Huron College. It had white cinderblock walls, fireproof curtains, and vomit-retardant carpet. Not the most romantic environment, but Jeff was in love. As with many of us, finding a good match wasn't easy for him. You could be standing in a backyard talking to Jeff and he'd spontaneously pick up a broken tree branch and run all the way around the house with his long brown hair fanning behind, pretending to search for water. Then his pasty, hairy, spindled legs would stop before you, where he'd drop the branch and act like nothing had happened.

Not all nineteen-year-old girls were drawn to his kind of quirk. But he found one who was—Michelle. The only problem was that she was in London, England, and Jeff was in London, Ontario. "I really miss her, but I don't have the money to go see her," he'd say each passing week.

One night, Jeff got into his rusty Chrysler K car, complete with a backfire and screeching fan belt, and drove two hours to the closest racetrack. He had never been to the horse races before, so he did some research and quick math to determine how much he needed to bet in order to win enough money to buy a ticket to visit Michelle. He put $20 down.

"I won $600—thirty times my bet!" He got to the point, not wanting to waste his winnings on long-distance phone charges to me.

"How the heck did you do that?"

"I won the trifecta. I guessed the order of the horses that would place first, second, and third. I hugged some dude standing beside me when my horses crossed the line." If you didn't excel doing permutations and combinations in high school, the odds of correctly guessing the first-, second-, and third-place finisher in a horse race with a field of twelve are long. When the odds are long, the returns for the lucky few are high. Jeff got lucky.

"So, I'm buying a ticket and I'm off to England. And I'm not telling anyone—especially not my parents. I'm just going to go." He knew the odds of them supporting his school-skipping trip to visit his girlfriend were longer than they are to win the trifecta.

Improving Your Odds

If you want to dramatically increase the returns on your speaking, you can win the Communication Trifecta. Three key things rarely show up in the same talk: expertise, experience, and personality. Winning the Communication Trifecta is neither risky nor difficult, it just takes planning. To win, you have to have all three of these elements, but they don't need to be in this order—so your odds are a lot better than Jeff's! If you follow the advice in this book, you are positioned to win—and win big, in a way that most won't.

As I noted earlier, if you solely focus on your expertise when speaking, you will limit the returns—like the aeronautical engineer who only talks about theory, such as pitch, drag, and roll. Technical and dry for most audiences, which makes it inaccessible and boring. As soon as you integrate examples and case studies into your talk, then you can reinforce the experience you have applying relevant theory successfully out in the world—Captain Sullenberger speaking about how to fly planes and handle emergency situations. The third component, personality, would seem to be the simplest, but is actually the rarest when people speak in high-stakes situations.

Putting Personality Front and Center on Stage

The Voice is a reality TV competition where aspiring unsigned singers vie to win US $100,000 and a record deal with Universal Music Group. The show combines performance, persuasion, and transformation—three things I love. The format includes blind auditions where contestants sing to four potential coaches who cannot see the performance but can hear the performer. Facing away from the contestant, the judges can only assess the voice, not looks.

If a coach likes a contestant's voice, they signal their interest by rotating their chair around to see the rest of the audition. If more than one coach likes the singer, they have to compete to persuade the performer to join their team of twelve artists. The coaches are accomplished musicians such as Blake Shelton, Alicia Keys, John Legend, and Kelly Clarkson. It's fun to watch superstars competing to convince amateurs to join their team.

Once on the team, the pros coach the amateurs on things like how to use their breath to hit a high note or how to change the arrangement of a cover song—"Let's try the snare on an off-beat"—to make it fresh. What may surprise you is how much of the coaching emphasizes the importance of getting their personality to shine through on stage.

"Don't over think, over feel," Pharrell Williams told one contestant. Singers are encouraged to think about how the song's lyrics connect with them on a personal level so they can convey that emotion to the audience through their own life experience. Aspiring musicians have dedicated years to developing their technical skills. Few have thought about or worked on ensuring their personality comes through during their performance, allowing them to build a strong connection with the audience and to move the room.

Does this sound familiar? Few of my clients have thought about how their personality can come through during their speaking. When they do, the result is dramatic. How can you do this? If you simply include a number of the Power Messages outlined in the preceding pages, your personality will almost certainly come along for the ride.

If you tell a story with emotionally charged dialogue—"That guy was so unbelievably arrogant that I will never hire anyone from that firm again!"—your personality will come through, particularly if your level of animation conveys the person's emotion. Then you can use a "Yikes" facial expression to show your reaction to the quote and add more of your personality.

If you use a vivid metaphor, your personality will come through too, as Atul Gawande's did when he said that cowboy specialists are disastrous, and that we need pit crews.

Even how you do a mic check is a chance to show more of yourself. How do most people do a mic check? "Testing, 1, 2, 3... Testing, testing, 1, 2, 3..." I've seen an all-star institutional investor say in front of an audience, "1 billion, 2 billion, 3 billion..." It was light-hearted and filled with personality.

Self-deprecating humor is another winning approach. "I know what you're thinking: 'How could someone who is five-foot-eight talk to you credibly about basketball?'" is a comment I've made to make light of my height, or lack thereof.

To win the Communication Trifecta you need to have the content *and* the ability to make it come alive through your delivery, which we will cover in the Close the Circuit chapter.

Set yourself up to differentiate—and win—by ensuring your expertise, experience, and personality show up when you speak.

4

USE ENABLING VISUALS

A T 7 PM on a warm September evening in 1994, Bev Rosser walked into a training room at SickKids Hospital with a seven-pound laptop under her arm. She plonked it on the table at the head of the room, making a louder thud than you want for a prized piece of expensive equipment—very few people had portable PCs back then.

A group of twenty had gathered to learn the ins and outs of being a volunteer on the oncology ward, where we were going to lead a weekly program of activities and crafts for the kids on 8A. Rosser has an energy and bright spirit that emanates from her even when she's not talking. The room went quiet as we watched her connect an octopus of cables to a projector. Our eyes widened as she tumbled through a series of slides complete with bullets pinwheeling in and checkerboarding out.

We'd never seen PowerPoint. We were dazzled like kids watching fireworks for the first time. But we didn't learn a thing about how to be a volunteer. We were too engrossed with the show.

Fireworks can be a great way to spark wonder and celebrate holidays, but in the wrong hands they can have unintended and disastrous consequences. The same is true for slides.

Slides are one of the worst things that has happened to face-to-face communication. It is not the software that's the problem, though; it's how it is misused. Too many people put too much content on too many slides, and then over-rely on them when they speak.

Here's a fun experiment: Get a friend or colleague who uses slides in a way that I've just described and ask them to present for two minutes as they typically do. Then ask them to present the same material but without slides. For the second take, tell them it's okay if they forget a few of the details—just ask them to get the big-picture ideas across. Film both versions and have your friend watch both. I'll bet the no-slide version is better.

In the decades I've been asking people who they think are impressive speakers and why, not once has somebody explained their choice by saying the speaker had amazing slides. Slides aren't the show—if they were, it would be called a slideshow. You and your story are the show, not the slides.

People invest an inordinate amount of time on their slides. Yet there are rapidly diminishing returns on slide prep time compared to focusing on preparing and delivering better content. If you are pressed for time, skip the slides. One in four of the Top 100 speakers doesn't use slides at all.

However, there are many good reasons to use slides and simple ways to use them more effectively. Let's explore a range of approaches you might take.

Differentiating in the Desert

"I still remember Nicolas's presentation on one of the most boring subjects one could possibly think about: 'Update on

the Sustainable Regional and Local Land Use Planning Act,'"
explained Louis about his partner Nicolas. Louis confessed
he'd wondered why he'd ever signed up to listen to the talk.
Nicolas followed two other presenters. "They gave classic presentations on similarly arid topics, the effect of which was to put
the entire room into a semi-comatose state," reported Louis.

Louis explained that Nicolas took an empathetic view and
considered the challenges faced by his audience. He focused
on what was important to them, not what was interesting
to him. "He knows he will never be JFK. But he also has an
ability to explain things clearly and simply, with a touch of self-
deprecating humor." Nicolas's humor can take you by surprise
because he looks at you and speaks to you with intensity.

He began by telling a story and involved the audience as
he told it. "He surprised us. He made us curious. He made us
laugh," reported Louis.

Nicolas eliminated all the details that weigh down most
decks. The slides were surprisingly simple—a phrase to distill the concept, a visual metaphor to represent an idea, a sole
number written in 800-point font. His slides weren't crutches;
they were part of a captivating story. He did not read them or
need notes because he knew his stuff. (I will address using
notes in the Close the Circuit chapter.)

He was the only speaker approached for follow-up discussion at the end of the event. "The clients were happy as much
with what they learned as how they learned it. With a little
bit of extra work and a different mindset, you can make a real
impact, even when you'll never be a Barack Obama. And that
pays big time," summarized Louis.

As we've seen with Nicolas, using slides can help you deliver
standout talks, but too often people make poor and counterproductive choices.

Use slides to enable your story.

The Waste of Cut and Paste

Jerry spun the two documents and slid them across the table. "Here's my white paper, and here's my presentation."

"They look the same. Verbatim. Are they the same?" I asked after doing a quick page flip.

"Well, my presentation is in PowerPoint—so that's different. But the content is the same." My client Jerry had cut and paste his white paper into slides and thought he could just read the deck to the audience. His paper had been well received when it was published, so why not replicate it, he thought.

While this is an extreme version of PowerPoint prep gone awry, many speakers' approaches aren't much better, and often can look like this:

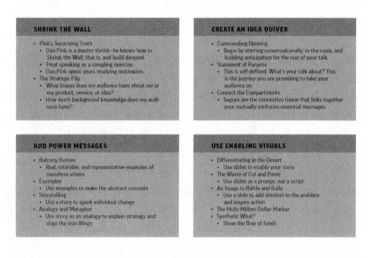

Too much material, tiny font, and lack of foreground and background contrast.

"I don't need to go to a conference to have someone read to me. I'm literate! Just send me the paper to read on my own and save me the trouble," is a complaint I've heard too often.

I also learned Jerry was afraid he was going to forget what he wanted to say. He'd never spoken to such a large audience before and figured he would use slides to reduce the chances of freezing and forgetting.

But what appears to be a safe approach can backfire. Avoid the trap of using your slides as a script. If you are afraid you will forget what you want to say, use your slides to prompt you.

I quoted Tom Peters in the storytelling section of the previous chapter. He's a Stanford PhD management guru and bestselling author who has been speaking to Fortune 500 audiences for decades, charging tens of thousands for the service. He is constantly updating his talk and slide deck. He makes his visuals available on his website.[1] His slides are useless, though. Useless to us, that is. They're useful to him. They prompt him. You'll see a slide with one or two words on it: "Private," "Jim's Group," "china!"

SOURCE: TomPeters.com/slides.

They won't win any design awards. But they don't need to. He's not selling graphic design. He's trying to communicate effectively, and he does. "Tom Peters is the Red Bull of management thinking," says author Bo Burlingham, and his slides energize him to deliver his talks.

If you don't think you're ready to abandon so much detail on the slides because you're fearful of forgetting what you want to say, remember that PowerPoint, Keynote, and Google Slides allow you to put speaker notes in a section below the slide. You can configure your display so that only you can see your speaker notes and your next slide. Of course, you'll still be able to see your current slide, too.

The Top 100 speakers use on average seven words per slide, not a wall of words. And they use more slides than you might expect—1.07 slides per minute.

At this point, you may be wondering about the usefulness of sparse slides if you also need to provide your listeners with a handout. I get asked this a lot. We will address that later.

Nicolas was inspired to change his approach when he saw a sample of Peters's slides. A simple change to how he used his visuals enabled—and differentiated—him as a speaker. It might just do the same for you too.

Use slides as a prompt, not a script.

An Image to Rattle and Rally

The Syrian refugee crisis had been going on for years and little had changed. Refugee camps were packed and growing. Foreign aid was static and insufficient. And options for a better future for hundreds of thousands of people had not improved. Until one photograph was taken and published throughout the world.

On September 2, 2015, sixteen people, including three-year-old Alan Kurdi and his family, climbed into an inflatable boat designed to carry eight. They had no life jackets when their boat capsized in the Mediterranean. After Kurdi drowned, the little boy's body was found and photographed by a Turkish press photographer.

The world had been failing during the largest humanitarian crisis in decades. But that picture of Kurdi put a face on the tragedy and incited people to take action. Within twenty-four hours of the picture being published, my chiropractor had joined a group of thirty associates and friends who were equally moved by the story. They committed to sponsoring a family. Days later they had raised $30,000, and within four weeks they had been matched with a family of seven refugees looking to start a new life in Canada.

They were one of thousands of Canadian groups who mobilized to do the exact same thing at the exact same time. All prompted by the confronting photo that summed up the horrors and sparked long overdue action.

If you want to get people to act—humanitarian crisis or not—try to find an image that encapsulates the problem and the need to change course for the better. Maybe it's a failing piece of equipment. Maybe it's a handwritten feedback form that says, "Whereas I would've considered using your firm in the past, now you're off the list." Maybe it's an image of a frustrated potter at the post office in Positano who wants to sell her ceramics in international markets and needs your platform to enable cross-border transactions. Showing an image of the problem is often more provocative than simply showing an image of the solution, because the problem creates tension.

Just over seven in ten of the slides used by the Top 100 speakers are image only—there is no text. The images visually reinforce the point, providing a thematic backdrop, but don't split the audience's attention between reading and listening. If you choose this approach, try to use high-resolution images that go right to the edge of the slide ("full bleed"). There are many great sites that provide high-quality, royalty-free images. Unsplash.com is one of my favorites.

Use a slide to add emotion to the problem and inspire action.

Enforcing the Code

If you worked in a large organization that had suppliers throughout the world, how would you manage these relationships to ensure your suppliers met your standards for things like quality control, ethics, and employee safety? Policies and procedures are a start, but are they enough?

Most organizations have them, and most of them are well meaning and thoughtfully crafted. Yet, most of these organizations also suffer a gap between having policies and people following them.

Sophisticated organizations that buy products from overseas have something called a Supplier Code of Conduct. Easy to have; hard to enforce. To encourage more enforcement, Parna, an expert in outsourcing contracts, put a full-bleed image of a collapsed factory up on the screen in front of an audience. "Does anybody know what this is?" she asked. A number of hands went up in the audience. "Isn't that Bangladesh?" offered one attendee as lots of heads nodded before the room went silent.

"That's right. This garment factory was illegally constructed and housed thousands of workers who were making garments for some of the world's top-tier brands. Most of these companies had Supplier Codes of Conduct. None of them actively audited their suppliers." Parna let the thought sink in before she continued. "Had they done so, the suppliers would have had to move to a properly built facility and 1,100 lives would have been saved." It was also not lost on this audience that the reputation of the brands who had been buying from this factory would not have been tarnished.

At the end of the talk, Parna was retained to assess one attendee's supplier agreements, policies, and audit procedures. Take out the image in the talk and I doubt she would've had the same uptake. When you can capture emotion in an image and use it to set up your solution, you can get your audience to take action.

To move people to act, show a visual of the underlying problem.

The Multi-Million-Dollar Marker

Robert was part of a complex accounting group—a Delta Force of sorts, only they used math instead of might. He was a member of a team pitching to win the work of a global engineering firm. If you've ever gone up the world's tallest towers or traversed the longest bridges, you're still alive because of their work. The engineers were frustrated with their incumbent accountant's ability to resolve complex accounting issues quickly and transparently.

"I anticipate you have the following three complex accounting issues based on a review of your last three annual reports," Robert said to the prospective client group. Their faces revealed the kind of wonder you see at the fair when a carnival worker accurately guesses someone's weight.

"Here's how I would work with you to resolve these issues," he continued. He proceeded to map out his process on a whiteboard. The client jumped in and asked a few questions. By the time he had finished, the tone in the room had shifted from crossed arms to open disclosures of additional thorny issues needing help. Robert's team won. During the debrief, the client said, "Robert won the work for you. He solved more in half an hour than the incumbent did in half a year."

The team shrank the wall and focused on relevant complex issues, and Robert used a $50 whiteboard and a marker to win a multi-million-dollar-a-year account.

Sometimes you don't need a fancy slide, just a whiteboard and a marker. And Robert.

Synthetic What?

When I have the opportunity to work with subject matter experts, I can typically understand the broad strokes of their content. Every once in a while, I'm way out of my depth. When I listened to Lise, I felt like I was bobbing around in the middle of the Baltic Sea. She was talking about how to use synthetic debt to create a total return swap. Exactly.

Speaking ten thousand miles a minute, which I'm sure is a fraction of her clock speed, she began to use slides to map out various entities and explain how funds and obligations would flow between parties. Unlike me, her audience was sophisticated tax practitioners. Yet even as a layman, I was able to grasp her explanation, at least at a superficial level. But remove the slides, and I'm back in the Baltic.

It's easier to explain complex structures with visuals. This is true whether you're a chemist explaining polar covalent bonds, a tax advisor outlining circular flow of funds, or a systems engineer showing the relationship between hardware and software.

If a picture is worth a thousand words, then diagrams are worth millions to fancy financiers advising on complex deals, structures, and combinations. Use 'em or lose 'em—your audience and the big bucks.

Show the flow of funds.

Anchor a Theme

Brent stood looking at the ad agency that he was charged to lead as their chief strategy and innovation officer. He's five-foot-nine, and less than 5 percent of his 140 pounds is fat. In other words, his stature defies the social science that shows a disproportionate number of leaders are of basketball-ready height. Yet you find yourself wanting to go for a drink with Brent even if you don't drink. He's clever, funny, and somehow manages to pull off wearing a scarf indoors.

He knew the leadership task ahead was going to be tough. The agency had lost a number of big accounts, and he'd inherited a senior team with some members who were apathetic at best and willing to sink others for personal gain at worst.

"This is us," he said, then paused as he turned around to look at the picture he'd revealed of a supertanker that was so big it couldn't fit in the frame on the massive screen behind him. He acknowledged all the great work that they had done for big and important clients. He lauded them for the awards they'd won and the recognition they'd achieved. Then he spoke candidly about their recent losses and struggles within the rapidly changing market.

"We don't just need to turn this ship. We need to lift it up out of the water and transport it to a completely different ocean. This will be far from easy. But it's necessary." He carried on, charting their course and showing the extraordinary opportunities ahead if they were successful.

His respect, frankness, and compelling vision won them over. Together they won new business in new sectors and providing new services. He led them to so much success in the new waters that he was promoted to run their flagship New York business. Rinse and repeat. He continued to advance through a series of increasingly prominent roles before returning to lead the Canadian business.

The full-bleed photo of the ship—branded, of course, with his agency's logo—allowed him to visually depict the metaphor and set the core theme for his talk. It was as vivid and memorable as were Brent and his vision. Find your ship.

Use bold, full-bleed visual metaphors.

Branding Bankruptcy

It was a cool morning in January 1997, and my friend Jonathan Baillie and I were wearing our newly purchased "hiking boots" (rubber boots) as we began our adventure among the hill tribes near Sapa, in northern Vietnam, at the edge of the Chinese border. "Why did you quit being a veterinarian to earn $10 a day being a guide?" I asked Tran as we descended the trail.

"I was tired of people bringing their animals to me when they were already dead," she said. People didn't understand what veterinarians did, much less the importance of preventive medicine. She got so frustrated with people coming to her when it was too late that she decided to quit ministering to dead animals and start taking foreigners on hikes.

Her frustration as a vet resonates with the many people in insolvency and restructuring work who I've met over the years. Managers of too many failing businesses don't seek help until it's too late—the corporate carcass is dead. Jason, an advisor in the space, had a chance to educate and encourage early intervention and create many win/wins.

Jason has a warm confidence and panache that shows up in big-knotted neckties and fashionably visible stitching on the lapels of sport jackets. While *he* can capture your attention when he speaks, his draft slides weren't setting him up for success. They were the standard six-bullets-a-slide snooze-inducing variety too many professionals tend to use. One slide summarized his most important takeaways: as the health of an organization declines, it goes through a number of stages; the time between each of these shrinks as things get worse; the tools available and the likelihood of resuscitating the organization shrink.

I challenged him to visually depict these insolvency steps, and he came up with the Solvency Curve. The Y axis depicted the health of the organization. The X axis depicted time. He plotted the stages of an organization's declining health and showed the shrinking space between the stages. Rather than relegating his role to that of a narrator and reading a bunch of bullets—and risk losing the audience's attention and more unnecessary corporate demises—he established his role as the primary storyteller and used the visual to explain the curve and the importance of early intervention.

THE SOLVENCY CURVE

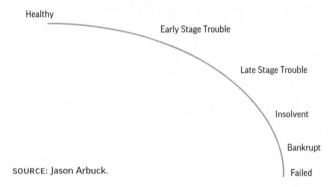

SOURCE: Jason Arbuck.

The print media in the room took note and approached him after the talk, resulting in a published piece on the Solvency Curve. This article was read by someone at the Business News Network, who invited Jason to talk about it on television. Jason's framework allowed him to explain and brand a key concept and raise his profile well beyond the conference room.

Try to visually depict your key concepts rather than recite a series of bullets.

Show the Spread

If you want to emphasize the folly of trying to time the market, use a line graph that shows the comparative performance of any major index and the same index with the top ten days of performance removed. The difference is typically between 60 and 70 percent. In other words, if you're not in the market, you're not going to benefit from its full potential. If you pull your funds out when you get nervous, you're likely going to miss the gains that will not only help you recover but ultimately grow your investments. Show a line graph of the spread between the market with and without the ten best days, and watch the loss aversion kick in for your listeners. Who wants to miss that 62 percent! Who said data couldn't tap emotions?

MARKET WITH AND WITHOUT TEN BEST DAYS

------- FINANCIAL TIMES STOCK EXCHANGE ALL-SHARE TOTAL RETURN
——— FINANCIAL TIMES STOCK EXCHANGE ALL-SHARE LESS TEN BEST DAYS

SOURCE: BMO Global Asset Management, March 2020, bmogam.com/gb-en/retail/wp-content/uploads/2020/03/ftse-all-share-1.svg.

Show the right lines to illustrate your storyline and add credibility.

Cutts's Rut-Breaking Recipe

Sometimes we can feel like our lives are in a rut. Matt Cutts did. His solution to get out? Try something he'd always wanted to try and do it for thirty days. He's a self-described computer nerd who appears to have traded in the masking-taped horn-rimmed glasses for wireless frames.

In his three-and-a-half minute TED talk, "Try Something New for 30 Days," Cutts rattled off some of his thirty-day experiments, each of which had a corresponding slide. "This was part of a challenge I did to take a picture every day for a month. And I remember exactly where I was and what I was doing that day." Above him stretched a photo of a moss-coated tree in a misty forest. It was a beautiful photo, but not so extraordinary that you wouldn't think you could take it. (Incidentally, research has shown that audience recall doubles when visual aids are used.[2])

When Cutts combines an idea (ride your bike to work), a corresponding image (action shot of happy Matt commuting), and the impact it had on his life ("My self-confidence grew"), he creates a persuasive packet. His images spark your imagination and prompt you to consider what you could try doing for thirty days, believe you can do it, and change your life for the better—exactly what he set out to do.

Visually depict examples to double the audience's recall.

Bad Math and Bad Slides

Be honest: What's one of the first things you do when you need to give an important talk? Do you open up your favorite slide software and start to make a deck? This is the equivalent of doing addition and subtraction before multiplication and division. You're setting yourself up for failure.

Do you remember BEDMAS? It is the order of operations that we learned in mathematics: brackets, exponents, division, multiplication, addition, and subtraction. If you follow the order of operations, you set yourself up to get the right answer. If you don't, you won't.

There is a similar order of operations in preparing to speak. As I've outlined so far: Shrink the Wall, create an Idea Quiver, add Power Messages, and *then* consider and create helpful visuals. Don't prep visuals first or you'll risk not getting an A. If you're the type who's reading this book, you don't like not getting straight As.

Follow the process: Shrink the Wall, create an Idea Quiver, add Power Messages, and then—and only then—create visuals.

Beware the Millstone of Handouts

At times you will be asked to have a handout. A simple and innocuous request. But it can set an unexpected trap. For the handout to be useful, it needs to be comprehensive. Once you've prepared a thorough handout, you may find yourself thinking you'll just use the same deck to project as your slides. After all, it reflects what you want to say and is thoughtfully written. What's the problem?

When projected, a comprehensive deck becomes a millstone that pulls you out of the room. You'll find it hard not to read or rely heavily on those well-crafted slides. Your eye contact will plummet and your vocal range will compress. Best case: your audience's attention drifts. Worst case: you lose credibility because it doesn't look like you know what you're talking about.

Remember Nancy's colleague who had people walk out of his presentation? That speaker read bullet after bullet after bullet.

How do you reconcile the need to have a handout with your desire to efficiently use your prep time and be engaging as a speaker? Here are three options.

1   **Bold the gold and hide the silver**—Prepare the handout deck first. Save it. Then save a new version where you will bold the key phrases—the gold—that you intend to elaborate on during the talk. There's no obligation to speak to every point that you put on the page. Having bolded phrases will help you and your audience quickly find the key point.

While you are elaborating on the gold, consider hiding the rest—the silver—so your audience won't get distracted reading it. They can read the whole document later. Your elaboration is likely going to be the most valuable part of your talk. It's where you will introduce your Power Messages.

Scott Miles, a creative pro and master presenter, has a great philosophy on using slides: every slide should have a "trapdoor"—a phrase or image that you will open up to reveal an interesting insight, example, stat, or story. The trapdoor could be the bolded phrase.

You don't want the audience distracted when you are talking about the treasure behind the trapdoor. To remove the distraction, press B on your keyboard when you are in slideshow mode. This will blank the screen. When you're ready to bring the screen back up, push B again. This works in all the major slide software programs. It also works when screensharing a video presentation. Try it.

Pro tip: When you blank the screen the first time in a talk, let the audience see it was your intention to do so. Look at the screen as you shut it off and appear calm, so they see you meant to do it. You don't want them to be worried the screen broke.

If you don't want to use the B key but you do want to manage the audience's attention, you might walk over to the slide and point at the gold phrase before walking away from the slide and elaborating on it while standing at a distance from the screen, say five to fifteen feet away. When it is time for your next point, walk back to the screen and point at the next piece of gold.

You don't always have to walk over to the screen to point at it, but sometimes it's nice to. The movement adds physical dynamism and directs the audience's attention. Other times it's helpful to guide the audience with phrases such as, "Second bullet . . ."

It doesn't cost anything extra to create another slide, so don't be afraid to turn one comprehensive slide into three separate ones. This will also help you keep your audience's attention with you in the room, in the moment.

Bold the gold.

2   **Thin to win**—Another option: Once you have bolded all the key phrases, you can simply copy and paste all the text that was on the slide itself and put it in the notes section below. Then delete all but the bolded phrases from the slide. Tell the audience at the beginning of the talk that they will get a comprehensive handout—the comprehensive deck you initially created—or the thinned-out slides with only the bolded phrases on the slides but with the detailed notes below the slides included in the material.

As I mentioned earlier, you can configure your display so that only you can see your speaker notes. The audience will only see the gold up top, not the silver stashed in the notes.

This approach requires only a bit of extra prep time, but it's time well spent. It encourages you to determine in advance what are the most important points that you will elaborate on in the room.

Put the details in the notes section, and place the thinned-out prompts on the slides.

3   **Create visual storyboards**—After you have bolded the key phrases, you could now consider adding an image that thematically represents the core problem or point that you're addressing on the slide. Search for a high-resolution image that you can either license or use royalty-free from a site like Unsplash.com. Copy and paste the image onto the slide, right click on it, and select "send to back." This will place the image behind your key phrase. Move the text around and change its color; create some transparent color fills to make the text more legible, if you know how and it would be helpful.

Complement the prompts with high-resolution images.

Don't Compete with Your Slides

As I mentioned previously, you are the show, not your slides. Don't demote your role to that of a narrator of bullets. This is particularly important at the beginning and the end of your talk. Do not change the slide the moment you begin to speak. "Good morning" + [click] = fractured attention. When you start, you want all eyes and ears on you, not your slide.

Separate your speaking-with-eye-contact from your pausing to reference your slides, and you will maintain your role as the primary storyteller. You will find it is easier to do this if you're standing on the left side of the slides (from the audience's perspective), as the audience reads from left to right. You want them to start by listening to you, then reading, then returning their eyes to you as they listen to you elaborate.

The same holds true for your close. Don't defer to a slide for your close. Finish strong by looking at your audience and speaking directly to them.

When you use slides while delivering online video presentations, be mindful that your video image gets reduced to one-tenth the size of the slide. Ideally, begin your talk without a slide so you can establish your digital presence. Learn how viewers can adjust their view to side-by-side and encourage them to use it. This way they can change the size to see more of you or more of your slide and get the most out of their experience. When you want to make an emphatic point, exit out of the slideshow mode so you're not competing with the visual.

Maintain your role as the primary storyteller.

For an infographic with the TED talk analysis ratios (per minute use of slides, stories, examples, and more), go to podiumconsulting.com/ratios.

5

CLOSE
THE CIRCUIT

Mr. Reckless Abandon Wrecked Himself

My colleagues and I were sitting in a hot, bright boardroom on
the corner of Church and Bloor in downtown Toronto in 1995.
We had been waiting eagerly for this meeting after spending
months working on rebranding our product and were excited
to see the new packaging concepts our ad agency had come up
with. "We approached this project with reckless abandon," said
the creative lead sitting across the table from us.

Everything looks in order if you just read his quote. But if
you were in the room, you wouldn't have been impressed. We
were insulted.

The creative lead would've sounded more excited if he
was talking about looking forward to shining his shoes, well,
if he had shine-able shoes. As he sat with his shoulders rolled
forward inside his retro Atari cool-guy T-shirt, he spoke in a
perfect monotone, avoiding eye contact like he'd just crashed
his mother's car and had to break the bad news. There was

nothing conveying the enthusiasm of the reckless abandon that he was declaring.

Maybe he simply wasn't proud of his work—we certainly weren't impressed by it. We didn't buy into him or his designs. We went across the street and found somebody who seemed to share some passion for their work—and for our project.

Mr. Reckless Abandon failed to close the circuit. He failed to align his content with his delivery and connect it to us— saying "reckless abandon" without a hint of enthusiasm or eye contact. It was a costly disconnect.

When the circuit is closed, the energy flows, the lights turn on, and you can move the room. A closed-circuit connection is rare. It is valuable. And it is powerful.

You can close it too. A few small changes can make a really big difference to the impact you have connecting with others.

So far we've talked about how to connect intellectually and emotionally with your audience through content—by Shrinking the Wall, creating an Idea Quiver, and adding Power Messages. Now we're going to focus on how you can Close the Circuit as you deliver these messages in the room.

Eye Contact

Social science has shown time and again that the most important delivery skill is eye contact. Even the most seasoned and accomplished speakers can improve their eye contact. Let's define the opportunity by looking at some data.

Researcher Carolyn Atkins wanted to understand how different amounts of eye contact affected audiences' perceptions of a speaker. She categorized eye contact in three levels: No Eye Contact—when a speaker looks at an audience for less than 10 percent of the time; Minimal—when a speaker looks at an audience 10 to 50 percent of the time; and Good—when a speaker looks at an audience at least 90 percent of the time.

Audiences don't think much of speakers who make minimal or negligible eye contact. Among the negative attributes they associate with these speakers—and the list is long—you will find "weak," "inferior," "dull," and "boring." None of us wants these words associated with us.[1]

When speakers hit the "Good," 90 percent threshold, audiences find them to be more likable and intelligent and judge them to be more deserving of a higher salary. Audiences learn more from these speakers.[2] That's a pretty attractive set of associations. Remember Luke's two-step process for easy change management in Chapter 1? Just make the status quo sufficiently uncomfortable and the proposed destination sufficiently attractive that people can't help but move away from the existing and toward the suggested place. I am optimistic you'll be inspired to move toward the "Good" level of eye contact!

Most speakers fail to hit 90 percent. They're not in the room. They're in their notes. They bring notes that are thoughtfully constructed and beautifully written. But then they over-rely on them, which pulls them out of the room. Remember the ballroom breaker whose monotonous technical talk helped birth my business? Not a great outcome—for him, anyway.

When I'm rehearsing with speakers who are over-relying on notes, I often will interrupt them and ask them a question. When they respond, they are in the room, making eye contact and speaking conversationally. Their colleagues watching inevitably say that their response to the question was stronger than the balance of their talk with notes.

I'm not against notes. I'm just against using them ineffectively in a way that pulls you out of the room. By all means have notes, but just pause to reference them. There's no need to try to be sneaky and hope your audience won't notice a furtive glance at a prompt you've written on your hand, like Governor Sarah Palin did when speaking to the Tea Party in February 2010. She had scribbled "Energy," "Budget cuts" (crossed out), "Tax," and "Lift American spirits" on her palm, which she referred to during the Q&A, leading to mockery after the event, particularly as she had just derided President Obama as a "charismatic guy with a teleprompter."[3]

That notes-on-your-palm strategy may have "worked" when writing a test, but it's not necessary when speaking. All you have to do is pause and calmly reference your notes on paper or a screen. Sounds simple, doesn't it? Here's the catch: when you are under pressure, you will not want to stop talking to look at your notes. It won't be long before you are starting and finishing many of your paragraphs speaking while you look down at your notes. This is not a conscious choice but a subconscious reaction to the stress when all eyes are on you. Heavy note-reliance is understandable, but it is suboptimal at best and counterproductive at worst.

If you're the kind of person who writes better than you speak, then script what you want to say as part of your prep process. It will be a good exercise to help you think through what you are going to cover and how you want to say it. Don't stop your prep there. Distill that script into bullets by bolding the key phrases in your script and then saving a new draft with nothing but the bolded bullets.

Then compartmentalize your bullets supporting an essential message in a box on the page so you can quickly find your next chunk of content when you briefly look down at your notes. In my simple learn-to-windsurf sample presentation, my first reason to try it is to enjoy the exhilarating experience of skimming across the water. Here's what my boxed bullets for that section might look like:

A. It's exhilarating to skim across the water

- create lift
- feel apparent wind
- compare to powder skiing
- Jeannie "got addicted to it; became a pro!"

Notice that the bullets don't need to mean anything to you as a reader. They mean something to me as the speaker. They are enough to prompt me to make my next point.

To maximize your in-the-room impact, stay with your current point until it is done. Your tendency will be to think ahead to your next point before it is time for it. For instance, based on my first windsurf bullets, imagine that while I'm *describing* how the board rises up out of the water as you pick up speed, I'm already *thinking* ahead to my next point about feeling the wind. When I do that, I pull myself out of the room and weaken the connection with the audience—and fail to Close the Circuit.

You've seen speakers who are ticking off the eye contact box, but you can tell they are in their head, searching their internal teleprompter to find their next point. Don't be that person.

Stay with your current point and look at your audience until it's done. Have faith that your next point is ready and waiting for you in your notes. Pause to reload your next point, and don't resume speaking until you've reconnected with your audience. As long as you appear to be calm when you reference your notes, the audience won't notice or will appreciate the break. You'll give them more time to think about your preceding point before you launch into your next one.

The same principles apply when speaking on video. Make eye contact with the camera lens for at least 90 percent of the time. Position your bullets just below the camera on a narrow, short page that you can scroll through. This will allow your eyes to stay close to the camera as you reference your notes. You can also place a sticky note with bullets on it just below the camera.

Ideally, you won't need to pause to reload more than once a minute. If you reference your notes more frequently, your presentation will drag. One of the benefits of Shrinking the Wall and adding Power Messages is you won't need to look at your notes as often as you would if you had a long series of bullets. Your content will be easier to remember.

If you forget what you want to say, calmly refer to your notes. The appearance of calm keeps the room calm and patient.

To move the room, you've got to be connected to the room at least 90 percent of the time. Pause to reload your next point.

Re-railing Your Train

Lizzie Velásquez, a Top 100 speaker, didn't have any notes when she described her experience in high school in "How Do You Define Yourself?" She'd found an eight-second video someone posted of her labeling her as the world's ugliest person. It had been viewed over 4 million times. Among the thousands of comments, she read, "Lizzie, please—please—just do the world a favor, put a gun to your head, and kill yourself."

Devastating. Then she'd had a realization: "My life is in my hands. I could either choose to make this really good, or I could choose to make this really bad. I could be grateful and open my eyes and realize the things that I do have, and make those the things that define me. I can't see out of one eye, but I can see out of the other. I might get sick a lot, but I have really nice hair." Someone in the audience called out, "You do! You do!" She laughed and then put her hands to her head. "You made me lose my train of thought!"

While this could have been a problem for many, it wasn't for Velásquez. She simply asked, "Where was I?" "Your hair! Hair!" they called out. She thanked them and carried on—no problem.

Even if you don't plan to use them, it's helpful to have notes close by, in your pocket, or sitting nearby on a table. Of course, they can be printed or on a laptop in front of you if you are using slides. Don't hold a phone or tablet in your hand as your notes. It will look like you jotted some ideas down while you were on the way to your talk.

Make typed bullets easy to read by bumping up the font size to 18 point or greater and only printing them on the top half to two-thirds of a page. Notes printed on card stock or cue cards won't exaggerate your shaking hands or ruffle in a microphone— a risk with regular paper. If you're using a lectern—and it's almost always better if you don't (details to come)—place your notes on it as high as you can, as close to the audience as possible. This will reduce the distance your eyes have to travel when it's time to look down and find your next point. You might need to use something to keep your notes from sliding back down toward you.

Number the pages. I've had a client drop her notes as she walked on stage. The cards weren't numbered, and they scattered on the floor out of order, adding a lot more stress to her day than she'd wanted.

Make small changes to your note prep so you can easily find your next point.

Connect Like a Pop Star

Now that we have your eyes up out of your notes, let's strengthen your person-to-person connection. Most speakers swirl and dart their eyes too quickly around the room, which makes them appear uncomfortable or nervous and weakens their connection. Don't. Instead, connect with each audience member for approximately three to five seconds. When you get to a comma or period in a sentence, move your eyes to randomly connect with the next person. The random shift is important—you don't want to systematically move from one person to the person right beside her, to the person right beside her—like a human sprinkler going "tik, tik, tik, shhhhhh, tik, tik..."

If you watch professional entertainers on stage, from Beyoncé to Bono, you'll notice their eyes are settled when they perform. Something you don't see in amateurs. The same is true for speakers. These pros weren't born on stage making great eye contact. They practiced.

Connect for three to five seconds per person before randomly connecting to the next.

Don't Confuse Awkwardness with Ineffectiveness

Now that I've given you a few delivery tips, it's time to anticipate how you will feel when you employ them: awkward. Change feels awkward. If you're not used to pausing to reference your notes, it will feel uncomfortable when you do. When I have people try this in front of their peers in my intensive small-group bootcamp program for speakers, they say, "That pause felt like an eternity." And their peers shoot back, "It didn't seem like it for us. It was much better."

When you consciously work on mechanics, you can look, well, mechanical. Don't abandon your efforts, though. With a little more practice, the appearance of mechanics fades and the presence of a stronger version of you comes to the fore. Let's say you are working on squaring your shoulders up to reinforce your eye contact as you randomly make connections around the room. It might look like you are doing the robot dance in your initial attempts. Stick with it a little longer and you will strengthen your connection with the audience and enhance your presence.

The path to effectiveness is through awkwardness.

Conversational Tone

Eloquence is a trap. If you seek it, you will likely pull yourself out of the room and into your notes. If you read, you will lose your eye connection with the audience and your vocal range will compress. Boring at best. Credibility-eroding at worst.

If your plan is to memorize, think again. If you memorize, the listeners will be able to see that you're not really with them but are reading along using the internal teleprompter in your mind. You will sound rote, not confident. Listeners will disengage and start preparing to-do lists in their heads.

Give up being eloquent. It's more important to *get the essence of the message across* while being in the room than it is to be eloquent. Distill your script to bulleted prompts. Then—and this is essential—give yourself permission to say it a little differently than the way you'd initially scripted it. In-the-room essence beats in-your-head eloquence 99.9 times out of 100. Chances are, you're not the one-in-a-thousand exception.

Now you're on your way to sounding conversational. The best speakers, like Brené Brown, sound conversational—like they're catching up with a friend—when they speak. Sure, their oratory may soar in moments, but they still sound conversational most of the time.

As soon as you give up being eloquent and focus on getting the essence of your message across, you will exceed the 90 percent eye contact threshold, and the eye contact benefits will accrue to you (more likable, more intelligent, judged to be more deserving of a higher salary). You will experience less stress. And you will sound more conversational, which is one of the subtlest ways to show confidence.

To help sound conversational, be sure to include some colloquial expressions that you use every day. One of my clients in the Southern United States says, "I'm fixin' to" when discussing her quarterly plans. In 2007, then senator Obama was "fired up and ready to go." Don't be afraid to use contractions. What sounds more conversational, "I am fired up" or "I'm fired up"?

Get the essence of the message across in a conversational tone.

Animating Your Hands and Voice

Too much of a good thing ceases to be a good thing. This is true for chocolate (I've tried), for wine (sometimes I forget I've learned this already), and for voice. If you continue to bump along in a conversational tone, you'll have a hard time keeping your audience engaged for a sustained period of time. To keep the circuit closed, switch it up. How?

There are a number of ways, including adding periodic slices of animation and authority to your voice. Look for emphatic statements and add vocal emphasis to them through your hands. Let's do a quick a/b test. Use the voice recorder on your phone and capture yourself doing the following:

a. Say, "This is a huge opportunity!" without moving your hands.

b. Repeat the statement, but this time gesticulate when you get to the word "huge." Pretend you're emphatically delineating the width of a fridge with your hands. Don't focus on your voice; focus on the physical commitment to the gesture: pretend there is a sheet of tissue paper in front of your body and move your hands with enough force to break the tissue paper. It's just an experiment, so don't be afraid to overdo the velocity of the movement.

Now play back the recordings and you will notice a dramatic difference in your vocal range. In the second version you will hear your voice pop with emphasis and authority, prompted by your hand movement. Imagine there is an invisible string and pulley system that connects your hands to your voice. The easiest way to open up your vocal range is to focus on your hands, not your voice. The voice follows the hands through the pulleys.

I'm on Fire Now

Picture a neuroscientist who works long hours and admits to having no social life. What comes to mind—bookish, rumpled, quiet? Wendy Suzuki, professor of neuroscience at New York University, appears to be none of these things.

She was on fire in front of a packed TED crowd, wearing cat-eyed glasses and a vibrant blue blouse. Her work has focused on the parts of the brain critical for the formation and retention of long-term memory. After years of immersion in this area, she did something rare for a tenured professor anywhere: she switched her research focus. She said, "I encountered something that was so amazing, with the potential to change so many lives, that I had to study it."

She explained that while her career was successful and she was becoming known in her field prior to the change, she was miserable. "I had no social life. I spent too much time listening to those brain cells in a dark room, by myself. I didn't move my body at all. I had gained twenty-five pounds."

To break out of the misery, she went on a river-rafting trip, "by myself, because I had no social life." After the audience laughed, she continued, "And I came back thinking, 'Oh, my God, I was the weakest person on that trip.'" So, she directed her type-A focus to exercise and noticed she had a great mood and energy boost and started feeling strong. This kept her going back to the gym.

A year and a half later, she'd lost the twenty-five pounds and noticed she was able to "focus and maintain my attention for longer than I had before. And my long-term memory—what I was studying in my own lab—seemed to be better in me. And that's when I put it together. Maybe all that exercise that I had included and added to my life was changing my brain. Maybe I did an experiment on myself without even knowing it."

Now Suzuki studies the life-changing benefits of exercise on the brain, which she champions as a certified fitness instructor. During her talk, "The Brain-Changing Benefits of Exercise," she filled the room with electric energy, which radiated from her arms and voice. The audience laughed when she said that the most common question people ask is what's the minimum amount of exercise you need to do to get the brain benefits. In response she said, "First, good news: you don't have to become a triathlete to get these effects." As she said, "you don't have to," she swept her hands like an umpire calling a runner safe at first— one of countless animations you'll see throughout her talk.

Toward the end of it, she got the audience to their feet to do a few simple aerobic exercises with some call and response. When she said, "I am on fire now," she pulled back her fist like a competitive athlete pumping her fist in victory. She definitely closed the circuit, with her energy magically conducted to the crowd, who responded with even more energy than Suzuki delivered. Within seconds, the whole room was ablaze. A moment after they sat down to let their fitness leader finish, they jumped back up in an ovation for her ideas and, no doubt, her energy.

Adding energy is even more important when speaking on video, which tends to flatten your delivery.

The Worst Advice

I hear this weekly: "But I was told many years ago not to move my hands because they are distracting." Yes, it is true that some people can use their hands with such frequency that they look like someone shooing flies at a picnic; however, rarely is this the case with definitive gestures, where the hands are aligned with your content. We'll get to non-aligned, unfocused hand movements in a minute, but you likely have lots of leeway to integrate some purposeful gestures that will add animation to your physicality and your voice without distracting your audience. "Don't move your hands" is generally bad advice. The majority of the Top 100 are moving more than half the time.

At some point you've likely watched an animated film (if you have kids, you've likely seen some of them one too many times!). Have you ever watched the voiceover actors record their work? There's some terrific footage of Cameron Diaz, John Lithgow, and Mike Myers performing their voice work for the movie *Shrek*. They all stand and use their hands demonstrably to bring their characters' voices alive. Of course, we cannot see them in the film, but we hear the animation in their voices.

One of my clients, Greg, used to speak in a narrow vocal range when talking about his international advisory work. He experimented with using more definitive gestures. He's a convert. Now every time I bump into him, he makes a point of giving me an animated hello. He snaps his arms open and says, "Trevor! Great to see you!" He looks and sounds so happy it makes me want to hug him.

The Easy Way to Add Authentic Color to Your Voice

If you simply try to add color to your voice, you will quickly sound like someone who is reading a children's story aloud and trying to make it sound interesting—a great strategy for the kindergarten classroom, not the boardroom. Focusing on your hands allows you to expand your vocal range authentically.

Our hands have so much to offer to our communication. Listen for verbal cues that could be supported by a definitive gesture. Here are six ideas to get you started:

1 **Enumerate**—When you tell your audience you want to share three key ideas with them, enumerate them by stabbing the air with an appropriate number of digits. Remember to use enough velocity in the movement to break that imaginary sheet of tissue paper. Don't point at your audience when you do this. Enumerating your content with gestures helps you deliver with clarity and conviction.

2 **Delineate items such as time, parties, or quantities**— If you're talking about something that happened over time, use an open palm chop to place the date on a horizontal timeline. Orient the timeline from the audience's perspective—from their left to their right, not yours. I've seen Doug McMillon, CEO of Walmart, use his hands to talk about wages and what he calls the ladder of opportunity. As he talked about different wages, he set them out with his hands on an imaginary ladder in front of him. A big part of his strong executive presence traces back to his hands and the authoritative tone of voice.

3 **Accentuate adjectives and adverbs**—Listen for descriptive words like "large," "small," "huge," "exploded," "grow," and "shrink," and match your gestures to them. You don't want to act out your presentation or look like you're playing charades. Capture the essence of descriptive words and phrases and convey them with your hands.

4 **Pause your hands in place to add emphasis and gravitas**— Top 100 speaker Esther Perel talks about the thorny topic of infidelity in "Rethinking Infidelity: A Talk for Anyone Who Has Ever Loved." She speaks with remarkable confidence. Her commanding authority is a combination of eye contact, emphatic pauses, and definitive-gesture-supported statements. "I look at affairs from a dual perspective: hurt [left hand moves out] and betrayal on one side [hand pauses], growth [right hand out] and self-discovery on the other [hand pauses]—what it did [left hand out] to you, and what it meant [right hand out] for me." Each key phrase is delivered to one person with eye contact. When she pauses, she keeps looking at the person who received the preceding point. Then she turns to the next person before she begins the next phrase.

   Too often people prematurely withdraw their hands, which dilutes their presence and minimizes their impact. Let's double down on our a/b test. This time, when you reinforce "huge" in "This is a huge opportunity," try a version where you pause your hands out front as though you're holding the imaginary fridge in space for two seconds, before lowering them. Compare that to a version where your hands drop before you get to the word "opportunity."

5 **Guide the audience's attention**—Use an open palm to direct your thanks toward the chair of the meeting who gave you the speaking opportunity, or point to the screen behind you when you want the audience to refer to it. Think of your hands as air traffic control for your audience's attention.

6 **Use your hands early in your remarks**— It will loosen you up and make you appear more comfortable and confident.

Sure, it's possible to overdo it. We all have a collection of informal and unfocused hand movements—a murky cocktail of Mr. Miyagi meets bouncing-ball-lyrical syncopation. This can make you charming in a conversation, but it makes it hard for people to take you seriously if you do it too much when you're presenting. If you have a lot of extraneous hand movement, give those hands a break and use them with more focus and purpose.

If you've been a quiet hand-talker, it may feel unnatural integrating some hand movement into your presentation. Try to use your hands next time you are on a conference call when no one can see you. Chances are, they will hear you with greater clarity, conviction, and authority, all led by your hands. And according to Suzuki, it will improve your brain function. If you want to ratchet your delivery up further, stand up to give your diaphragm a chance to boost your projection.

Expanding your vocal range by animating your hands is a powerful way to switch up your delivery.

We'll explore ways to expand your vocal repertoire as we continue through this chapter. First, let's finish up with the hands. You won't want to use your hands all the time, so what do you do with them when you are not using them?

Composure, Hands Edition

I'm often asked, "What should I do with my hands when I'm not using them?" People don't know where to put them. It's funny—we've had these appendages stuck to our torsos for decades, and for the most part, they don't cause us problems. Yet as soon as we stand up in front of an audience, the arms and hands seem alien and awkward.

You have a few options. You can rest them together in front of your navel. When you do, loosely interlock your fingers or have the back of one hand in the palm of the other, or simply have a couple of parts of each hand casually touching—just ensure you don't show tension in your hands by gripping tightly.

Avoid resting your hands together and low, as you would if you were naked and feeling exposed. This will roll your shoulders forward and down, diminishing your presence. If your hands are in front of your navel area, your shoulders will roll back slightly, which will enhance your presence. This is the go-to position for countless executives, like Facebook's Sheryl Sandberg and Walmart's Doug McMillon. The same is true for TV journalists like CNN's Anderson Cooper and CBC's Ian Hanomansing.

A variant of this is to imagine you're holding a cafeteria tray and rest your hands with your elbows by your side. This approach can work well if your arm-length-to-waist ratio makes it harder to comfortably have them meet in the middle and touch.

Avoid the at-ease rest position. Ironically, you don't look at ease. You look like a stiff who's nervously waiting to meet royalty. And no hitching the pants or skirt, unless of course you're staking your claim in a saloon. Keep your clothes up with tailoring and a belt.

I also suggest you avoid having your arms hanging by your side. You'll lose the rolled-back shoulders and will look rigid at best and like a Neanderthal at worst, not poised.

To round out the set of hand-related distractions, avoid digging around in your pockets. We are getting to the point where we live in an almost keyless and changeless world—thankfully—and there's nothing left to jingle. So remove the temptation if you're a reforming jingler. A hand in the pocket is fine if you're talking in a more informal context, just don't use your pockets to solve the problem of not knowing what to do with your hands.

Aim to have your hands resting for approximately 10 to 20 percent of the time you are speaking. Remember, as you explore using and resting your hands more purposefully, you may feel awkward. Don't confuse the feeling of awkwardness with ineffectiveness. Practice resting your hands when you are in a comfortable setting to get used to it, so your hands know what to do when you're under pressure.

Rest your hands together in front of your navel to elevate your composure.

Framing, Light, and Sound for Video Talks

When speaking on video, it would be a shame if you've added some nice animation but people couldn't experience it. Make a few adjustments to make the most of your online talks so you can strengthen your digital connection. Here are three tips:

1   **Shoot for a better angle**—Position the camera at or just above eye level for a more flattering angle. You can place your laptop on boxes to adjust the height. If you use a phone, it will be helpful to have a mini-tripod or tripod and a mount to attach your phone to the tripod. Frame the shot so you have, at the very least, your head and upper torso in the frame. This way you'll be close enough for a strong connection while still keeping some of your gestures in the shot. Try to have a clean, uncluttered background to minimize distractions.

2   **Make the light just right**—It helps to have a primary source of light, called a key light, and a secondary source, called a fill light. The key light can be natural light from a window.

Preferably it will hit your face on a forty-five-degree angle. This will create some shadow on the other side of your face. A bit of shadow helps create definition, which is good. If there's too much shadow, you can use a fill light to reduce the contrast. Avoid sitting in direct sunlight or placing yourself too close to a bright window as it will wash you out. You can put a layer or two of paper over a window if the light is too bright.

3 **Support your sound**—Carpet, furniture, curtains, and bedspreads absorb sound and help dampen potential echoes. A few dollars on a mic will markedly improve your audio. Place the mic close—six to twelve inches from your mouth— to get the technology working for you.

Make small changes to how you look and sound when speaking on video.

Pace and Pause

"I was told early in my career that if I speak faster people will think I'm smarter," Khalil told me in a brown carpet-tiled meeting room in a two-story hotel with partitioned walls. We were there to do the immersive speaker bootcamp program with his colleagues.

"Who told you that?" I replied. He couldn't remember. I suggested that he was robbing people of the opportunity to appreciate the value of his creative ideas.

"So what should I do?" he asked. "I know I should slow down, but I can't. And I love getting people excited about ideas!"

Khalil is not alone in his rapid-pace dilemma. The average Top 100 speaks at 165 words per minute. New Yorkers are particularly speedy talkers at 200 words per minute.[4] The Top 100 speed-talkers are Shawn Achor and Tony Robbins, at 230 wpm and 231 wpm, respectively. When I watched Achor's talk, I had to check to see if I'd left my playback settings at 1.5x speed. I hadn't.

"I write 'SLOW' on my notes as a reminder to slow down," is a strategy I hear from folks who've been trying to slow their pace down. "How does that work for you?" I ask. Nine times out of ten, the person says it doesn't. "I sound like a robot and I revert to my speedy delivery," they reply. Or, "I forget to notice the word once I start the talk."

I told Khalil, "Audiences love you in part because of your infectious energy, which gets conveyed through your rapid pace. Keep it." He looked momentarily confused until I continued, "And complement it—offset your rapid pace with more frequent and longer pauses." I paused to let the idea sink in.

"The audience can use the pause to process and delight in the idea you just shared before you get them excited about your next one." He's a fan of the arts, so I added, "Imagine I put you in a wheeled office chair and pushed you around the MOMA while I ran and said, 'Quick, look, there's a Monet there and a Matisse there and a Van Gogh there.' How far do you think I'd get before you shouted, 'Stop! I want to take the work in'? Let your audience take your work in."

The notes I handle no better than many pianists. But the pauses between the notes—ah, that is where the art resides.

ARTUR SCHNABEL, PIANIST AND COMPOSER

It's easy to think about pausing. It's hard to do it. Here are some ways to pack in more, punch up your delivery, and keep the circuit closed.

Want to Know One Way to Prompt Yourself?

Pressure tends to accelerate our pace, not slow it down, so pausing becomes more important when you're feeling tense. What can you do to prompt yourself to pause and offset your rapid pace? Use some rhetorical questions to nudge you to hit the brakes. As a bonus, you will further engage an audience, as it's almost impossible to ignore rhetorical questions, isn't it?

Top 100 speakers use a rhetorical question every other minute. In "The Price of Shame," Monica Lewinsky told the TED crowd in Vancouver in March 2015 that a twenty-seven-year-old at another conference had tried to pick her up. "He was charming, and I was flattered, and I declined. You want to know what his unsuccessful pick-up line was?" She paused for over two seconds as she lured the audience in. You could almost feel them lean toward her in anticipation. "He could make me feel twenty-two again."

Pause after rhetorical questions.

Count the Ways

Enumerate and pause after the numeral. When I was working at Heinz, Bill Springer was the president of North American operations. He paused after "First," when he said, "There are six things and six things only we are going to focus on in the coming year. First . . . tuna."

Build the habit of pausing after numerals, to let your point linger longer.

Stick Your Neck Out

Elevate and isolate your headers and sub-headers with pauses. Here's how Springer used pauses to elevate his header: "First, [pause], tuna [pause]." As you can see, he paused on both sides of his header, "tuna." Lift your headers up from the balance of your talk by placing pauses on either side of them. This will add clarity and offset your faster delivery when you elaborate.

Pause after stating headers.

Win Like the Gipper

Use some short sentences. Pause after them. Experts can quickly spin their prose to include multiple subordinate clauses. Add this tendency to fast talking and you have a recipe for losing your listeners. Be sure to include some short sentences during your remarks. Try to cut down long ones. Ask, "How would Hemingway say it?" Ronald Reagan used short, punchy statements throughout his presidency, including when he was running for re-election in 1984. During his campaign, he distilled the optimistic promise of his leadership to, "It's morning again in America." He won.

Pause after short statements.

If you prompt yourself to pause using the tactics above, you'll more sustainably and consistently offset your rapid pace and slow down the overall flow. Keep the energy that can be conveyed with rapid pace, just add some offsets. As a bonus, the pauses will build your gravitas, which we will explore next as you start to combine pausing with other elements of power.

Pause after Emphatic and Emotive Points

B.J. Miller is a hospice and palliative care physician and counselor at Mettle Health in San Francisco. He came to his work through a traumatic experience that almost took his life. After a night of drinking with a couple of friends when he was a college sophomore, at 4 am he climbed on top of a parked commuter train. He was the first to make it to the top. When he did, 11,000 volts of electricity arced from some equipment to his watch.[5]

He woke days later in the nearby burn unit, where he underwent months of treatment and multiple surgeries. He's now a triple amputee. This experience gave him insight into the structure of our care system.

The system is full of good, exceptionally talented people, some of whom are responsible for saving his life. It's also flawed. For Miller, the disease orientation of healthcare design is bad design. This is most apparent at the end of life, where there is a concentration of care. Instead, he believes healthcare design should be people centered.

Twenty-five years after his accident, he sat in front of a still crowd in green chairs arranged in concentric circles around the TED stage. In "What Really Matters at the End of Life," he invited the diverse audience to contribute to the bigger design conversation about how to bring intention and creativity to the experience of dying. Miller provided three design cues to rethink and redesign how it is we die, one of which is to allow for a sense of wonderment and spirituality. Research shows it is one of the things that's important to us as we approach death. To illustrate that beauty can be found anywhere, he recalled a snowy evening that arrived months into his care in a burn unit of Saint Barnabas Medical Center in Livingston, New Jersey. As he overheard nurses complaining that it was difficult to drive through it, he could only imagine the sticky snow because he was stuck in a windowless room.

The next day, one of his nurses smuggled in a snowball for him. "I cannot tell you the rapture I felt holding that in my hand, and the coldness dripping onto my burning skin; the miracle of it all, the fascination as I watched it melt and turn into water. In that moment, just being any part of this planet in this universe mattered more to me than whether I lived or died. That little snowball packed all the inspiration I needed to both try to live and be okay if I did not. In a hospital, that's a stolen moment."

Miller's a Top 100 speaker, and it's easy to see why. He lets extraordinary moments like this breathe with beautifully placed pauses. I will show them in brackets here. As you reread the passage, pause to reflect on Miller's message where he pauses:

> I cannot tell you the rapture I felt holding that in my hand [pause], and the coldness dripping onto my burning skin; the miracle of it all, the fascination as I watched it melt and turn into water [pause]. In that moment, just being any part of this planet in this universe mattered more to me than whether I lived or died. That little snowball packed all the inspiration I needed to both try to live and be okay if I did not [pause]. In a hospital, that's a stolen moment [pause].

Design can allow for sensuous gratification, where we can be rewarded in a moment for just being. Miller suggested that one of the most important rooms in the hospice guest house is the kitchen, which is unexpected given many residents eat little, if anything. He explained that the kitchen provides sustenance on many levels, including smell and what he described as a symbolic plane. "Seriously, with all the heavy-duty stuff happening under our roof, one of the most tried and true interventions we know of is to bake cookies." Then he paused—*for twelve seconds*—before continuing. It's our senses that connect us and make us feel human, and in the case of cookies, accessing just one sense—smell—is enough.

Miller told the audience that parts of him died many years ago. He gestured toward his prosthetic legs as he acknowledged that we all experience loss. "I got to redesign my life around this fact, and I tell you it has been a liberation to realize you can always find a shock of beauty or meaning in what life you have left, like that snowball lasting for a perfect moment, all the while melting away. If we love such moments ferociously, then maybe we can learn to live well—not in spite of death, but because of it." He paused for three and a half seconds before finishing. "Let death be what takes us, not lack of imagination."

Take a moment to reflect on how you think the audience responded.

Pause for the cause. Design moments of reflection into your talks.

The right word may be effective, but no word is ever as effective as a rightly timed pause.

MARK TWAIN

Power Pauses Compound Your Power

If you want to add more weight to your speaking, first you need to have something to say. We've covered that. Then you need to say it like it matters. It's not enough for *you* to know what your important points are, you need to signal to the audience which ones are most worthy of their attention and consideration. Pausing is a powerful start—and you can do more.

When you start to layer a few delivery skills together, they compound in their impact. For example, if you make a concise, emphatic statement while making eye contact with one person, and pause while maintaining your eye contact with *the same person*, you multiply the power ascribed to the point. I call this a Power Pause. Facts presented just before a pause have higher recall than other points, so be sure to add one after your important gems.[6]

There's a scene in the TV series *The West Wing* in which President Bartlet is talking to his daughter Zoey, a high school senior, in the Oval Office the day after her security has been compromised when she was out with overdressed senior staffers at a college bar.

When Bartlet tells Zoey she'll have a bigger security detail when she goes to college in the fall, she protests. She says the Secret Service is too busy being worried about him getting shot. He says that's nothing compared to how terrified they are of her getting kidnapped. He describes a scenario where she gets abducted and taken hostage overseas, at which point he almost shouts in distress, "This country no longer has a commander-in-chief, it has a father who's out of his mind because his little girl is in a shack somewhere in the middle of Uganda with a gun to her head." Then he pauses before asking, "Do you get it?" with the full emotion of a parent imagining their child whose life is in danger.

He says these lines while looking at Zoey, and he *keeps looking at her* during the whole eight-second pause that follows. It's a powerful scene. Reduce the pause or remove the eye contact and the power dissipates.

Let's try a Power Pause. Think of something that you recommend people do that will positively change their lives. Create a concise summary of the recommendation; for example, "Learn to windsurf and you will experience the thrill of living in a new way." Then record yourself doing two takes:

1   Deliver the line with your eyes sweeping around the room.

2   Deliver the line with eye contact to one or two fixed points in the room, assuming the points serve as placeholders for people (I assume you're alone). For instance, a light switch and a door handle could serve as focal points to represent two listeners.

For the second take, in my sentence I'd deliver "Learn to windsurf" looking at the light switch, say, and pause as I turn to the door handle and say, "and you will experience the thrill of living in a new way." And I would pause after "new way" while still looking at the door handle. If you were to elaborate on your recommendation, you'd move your eye contact to a third focal point when you continue *after* the Power Pause.

You can apply the same approach to great effect when delivering a series of thought-provoking questions. Esther Perel does this when talking about infidelity. As a practicing psychotherapist, she has found that often people in affairs aren't "looking for another person, as much as [they] are looking for another self."

In her talk, she explained that affairs often follow a recent loss such as the death of a loved one "because they raise questions." For each of the following questions, she looked at one person, delivered it with eye contact, and paused for a moment, holding eye contact with the same person, before turning to the next one:

- Is this it? [pause with eye contact, then turn to the next person]

- Is there more? [pause with eye contact, then turn to the next person]

- Am I going on for another twenty-five years like this? [her eye contact wavers a bit]

- Will I ever feel that thing again? [pause with eye contact, then turn to the next person]

Perel thinks that "perhaps these questions are the ones that propel people to cross the line, and that some affairs are an attempt to beat back deadness, in an antidote to death." She hears from people all over the world that the affair made them feel alive. She makes it clear she is not "for" affairs, no more than she is for cancer.

When you experience her speaking, you feel the force of her presence and the strength of conviction through her

Power Pauses. Too many people cut their pauses too short after emphatic statements and inadvertently lose power and gravitas as a result.

Maintain your eye contact through the pause and you'll compound your power.

Charisma Killers—Disfluencies and Filler

People's definitions of charisma vary, but research finds charismatic speakers are commonly found to be enthusiastic, charming, persuasive, passionate, convincing, and not boring. This book is building you up to be more charismatic. Suboptimal delivery can rapidly erode the charisma you've worked hard to create.

The quickest way to destroy your charisma is to add disfluencies—they're the kryptonite of charisma. Disfluency is the interruption of fluid speech, which includes the use of "um" and "ah," repeated words, and restarted sentences. Disfluencies are negatively correlated with being charismatic—the greater the disfluencies, the lower the charisma rating. The presence of disfluencies conveys a lack of clarity and reduces people's perceptions of your confidence in your message, which undermines your ability to be convincing.[7]

How many disfluencies do you think there were in all the presidential inaugural addresses between 1940 and 1996? There were 125,950 words spoken across all the speeches during this fifty-six-year period, and there were no disfluencies. None.

Many speakers are unaware of their use of "um" and "ah" and qualifying phrases such as "kind of" and "sort of," which make them sound uncertain. Let's use the term "filler" for this collection of diminishing and distracting sounds. The easiest way to find out if you use fillers is to record yourself speaking and count how many fillers you use in a minute.

As a benchmark, the Top 100 use just over two every minute. If you speak English as a second language, you may be inspired to learn that the Top 100 who are ESL use fewer fillers than the native English speakers.

If you want to reduce your use of fillers, rather than focusing on removing a negative—the filler—try to create something positive—silence. For most people, the act of creating more pauses has the effect of reducing fillers. As you experiment with this, try to pause where you would have a comma or a period if the sentence were written.

Replace the potholes in your prose with pauses.

Uncertainty and Upspeak

Many people end statements with their intonation rising. Imagine I were to say to you, "I'm so happy to be here?" in an interrogative tone. You wouldn't believe me because of the "upspeak" inflection. Upspeak is characterized as incomplete, inconclusive, and anti-assertive, because your intonation is rising.[8]

Research finds that when people make incorrect statements, their intonation rises 64 percent of the time, compared with only 33 percent of the time when the answer is correct.[9] So listeners are right to assume upspeak is associated with a lack of confidence in your content.

Finish on a flat to declining tone, and you will add to your gravitas and engender more confidence in your listener.

Reference Back

People often ask me, "What are some of the things that the best speakers do and the rest of us don't?" One answer is that they show they are in the room by referring back to things that people have recently said. They do this on stage or in the boardroom without having had the opportunity to plan these remarks in advance. When Sir Ken Robinson gave his first TED talk, "Do Schools Kill Creativity?" he referenced back to a young musician's performance from the night before: "We've all agreed, nonetheless, on the really extraordinary capacities that children have—their capacities for innovation. I mean, Sirena last night was a marvel, wasn't she? Just seeing what she could do. And she's exceptional, but I think she's not, so to speak, exceptional in the whole of childhood … And my contention is, all kids have tremendous talents, and we squander them, pretty ruthlessly."

One of my friends was in a town hall meeting in the United States during a presidential primary contest. Five community leaders spoke, and then one of the presidential candidates got up to address the crowd who had gathered in a barn in rural America. At various points during his remarks, the candidate referred back to something that each of the five community leaders had said earlier that night. The crowd was mesmerized—and not just this crowd. So was the nation, who decisively picked him as their president. I've seen presidents representing both sides of the aisle use this technique in a way that most speakers don't.

What we often get is the opposite. "It is surprising to see so many of you here on time, so early in the morning after a fun night out in the city," remarked a leader in a hotel ballroom in Montreal at 9 am on Saturday. There's nothing wrong with the content. The problem is that he read it. The comment was intended to sound like an in-the-room observation but came off as disingenuous.

Another leader knew better. "It's so great to be with you all here this evening. Let's pause for a moment to thank our catering manager, Derek. Derek, you have outdone yourself yet again this year. I was passing by a table of hors d'oeuvres and I heard Gail remark, 'My goodness, this wheel of shrimp is bigger than a wagon wheel. I've never seen such a beautiful display of seafood in my life.' There are 400 happy people here tonight. Their good spirits are largely a credit to you as you've fed us so well, as always. Thank you."

The Gail reference was not planned. It was a genuine, ad lib remark that added more weight to his thanks and created a nice in-the-room moment.

Reference back to show you are listening. It will also prompt you to sound conversational and Close the Circuit.

Interaction

Say "Aye"

If there were a walk of fame for speakers, one of its first inductees would be Tony Robbins. That man can move the room. It's no surprise that he's in the room to a greater extent than any of the other Top 100.

"When you fail to achieve, what's the reason people say? What do they tell you?" he asked the TED audience in "Why We Do What We Do." This wasn't a rhetorical question. He prompted them with, "Didn't have the..." and got them to complete the answer. We hear knowledge, money, time, technology, manager. Then we hear an answer he wasn't expecting: "Supreme Court."

Robbins smiled and pointed at the speaker while repeating, "The Supreme Court." He jumped off the stage and walked toward the man with a rat-a-tat-tat laugh before giving him a high five. It was Al Gore. The audience burst into cheers and applause for Gore's reference to his loss in the 2000 presidential election based on the Court's decision.

Robbins returned to the stage and waited for the room to settle before explaining that people say they are missing resources, but the defining factor is lack of resourcefulness. He told Gore that if he had used more emotion in his campaign, he would have won the 2000 election. The room erupted again, some shouting, "Yeah!"

The exchange between Robbins, the audience, and Gore continued as Robbins suggested the role emotion could have played in determining the outcome before asking, "Do you know what I'm talking about? Say, 'Aye.'" The audience enthusiastically responded in unison and conviction. Robbins's in-the-room connection created a tight circuit. It's a marvel.

You may not have Al Gore in your audience, but you don't need him to get some audience interaction. This engagement is even more important for keeping a remote audience connected when speaking on video. It can be as simple as doing a live show-of-hands poll. "Raise your hand if you've ever worked in an organization that's experienced a cyber breach." Then make a quick, in-the-room observation or two: "Looks like about half. Based on your facial expression, Amanda, it doesn't look like it was an enjoyable experience..."

Interact with your audience to engage them, pull you into the room, and Close the Circuit.

Add Levity

Psychologist Shawn Achor is an outlier who studies outliers. He's an academic who is funny.

Achor generates more laughs per minute than almost any of the Top 100—almost two per minute. He's only outdone by Mary Roach's titillating topic of orgasm, which teased out lots of teenage I-can't-believe-I'm-hearing-this giggles.[10] In "The Happy Secret to Better Work," Achor has almost four times the laughs as the Top 100 cohort's average, part of which may be explained because he speaks so fast and can pack in more material during his allotted time.

He thinks we've got it wrong with success and happiness. On a May morning in 2011 in Bloomington, Indiana, Achor recounted to a crowd a conversation he had had with leaders of a prestigious boarding school in New England. They were excited to tell him about their annual wellness week: "Monday night we have the world's leading expert to speak about adolescent depression. Tuesday night it's school violence and bullying. Wednesday night is eating disorders. Thursday night is illicit drug use. And Friday night we're trying to decide between risky sex or happiness." The audience laughed.

Achor followed up by saying, "That's most people's Friday nights." This time the audience laughed and then applauded his humor. He was killing it.

Then he made an in-the-room comment: "I'm glad you liked [what I said], but they did not like that at all. Silence on the phone. And into that silence I said, 'I'd be happy to speak at your school, but that's not a wellness week, that's a sickness week. You've outlined all the negative things that can happen, but not talked about the positive.'"

As a positive psychologist, he explains why our thinking is flawed. If you work harder, you think you'll be more successful and then you will be happy. But every time you achieve a milestone, your brain advances the success goalposts. If happiness is always on the other side of moving goalposts, you will never reach it.

He advocates for switching the sequence. If you start with a positive brain state, you will perform significantly better than when you're negative, neutral, or stressed. He uses data to back this up and shows that your intellect, creativity, and energy rise when you are in a positive state. And he uses humor to lift you up in the moment and keep the circuit closed. It's no wonder he makes such an impact with his speaking. That's a powerful blend.

Clients often ask me about the importance of humor. It's nice to have, but not necessary to be a great speaker. Humor is a great way to snap the audience's attention back and keep the circuit closed. Research has found that humor helps keep students engaged, but it doesn't improve their grades.[11] If you are considering incorporating some humor, here are three questions for you:

1   Are you funny? When you go for laughter do you get silence, groans, or laughs? If your answer is A or B, your humor isn't stage-ready.

2   Is humor appropriate for this audience? Too many of us have seen a speaker try to land a joke that may have worked in the bar or locker room but isn't appropriate for the boardroom.

3   Is humor appropriate for your topic? If you're giving a talk about infant malnutrition, your ability to go for laughs is limited. If you're talking about the ways in which the education system is failing children, you may have some more to work with. Sir Ken Robinson did that brilliantly in his hilarious TED talk.

If you can't confidently answer yes to all three of these questions, your attempt at humor will likely hurt more than help. Everyone knows when you are going for a joke, and everyone knows when it fails. Nothing kills your confidence faster than a botched attempt at humor.

If you are simply trying to lighten the tone, you're not susceptible to the binary judgment of laughter. The tone-shift is another tool in your kit to keep the circuit closed.

Aim for levity, not laughs.

The Short of It

Nothing endears you to people more quickly than making light of some of your imperfections. When I talk about presence in front of an audience, I frequently make fun of the fact that I'm a short dude and need all the help I can get on the presence front—without platform shoes, thanks. The self-deprecating truth can lift the mood, generate empathy, and make you approachable.

It did for writer Isabel Allende when she said to a TED audience, in "Tales of Passion," "Allow me to tell you about my four minutes of fame. One of the organizers of the Olympic ceremony, of the opening ceremony, called me and said that I had been selected to be one of the flag bearers. I replied that surely this was a case of mistaken identity, because I'm as far as you can get from being an athlete. Actually, I wasn't even sure that I could go around the stadium without a walker." You can't help but like her more after her humble self-assessment.

In setting up a talk, Dan Pink shared some of his academic background: "When I got to law school, I didn't do very well. To put it mildly, I didn't do very well. I, in fact, graduated in the part of my law school class that made the top 90 percent possible. I never practiced law a day in my life; I pretty much wasn't allowed to." Pink's willingness to poke fun at his academic performance shows us that self-deprecating comments are a sure-fire way to lift the mood in the room.

Make light of your shortcomings—just don't undermine your credibility.

Our Listener in Wisconsin

The podcast cohosted by best friends Jason Bateman, Will Arnett, and Sean Hayes has enjoyed a meteoric rise based on the blend of star power, playful repartee, and humility. It's called *SmartLess*, a title that humbly under-promises for a show whose hosts and guests are a who's who of the zeitgeist.

"For our listener in Wisconsin, when Will says, 'Arrested,' he's referring to the show *Arrested Development* that he was in," Sean might say. On almost every episode, they refer to their single listener, Sean's sister in Wisconsin, as though this bunch of goofballs could only manage to capture one pair of ears in podcastland when they're actually one of the top ten shows in the world.[12] This is one way they keep themselves and the show grounded.

Use humility to add humanity and levity. It's smart.

Play with Stereotype

"Now, you've listened to me, and I know what you're thinking: She has a French accent, she must be pro-affair," Esther Perel said toward the close of her talk on infidelity. "So, you're wrong. I am not French." The audience laughs and applauds before she adds, "And I'm not pro-affair."

Her comment works because of the well-known history of infidelity in France, including the publicized extra-marital affairs of past presidents.[13] It works because of the surprise: while Perel has a French accent, she's not French—she's Belgian. And because she was going for levity, it would have worked had the audience not laughed.

If you are going to make light of a stereotype, it's best if you are a member of the group that's the subject of the comment. And, of course, your remarks cannot be unduly harsh.

Toy with innocuous stereotypes.

The Nub of Truth

After seven years of research on work-life balance, Nigel Marsh summarized what he'd learned to the TED audience in "How to Make Work-Life Balance Work": "There are thousands and thousands of people out there leading lives of quiet, screaming desperation, where they work long, hard hours at jobs they hate, to enable them to buy things they don't need, to impress people they don't like." When he said this, the audience laughed as they acknowledged the sad truth of his observation. By the time they'd finished laughing, they'd started applauding before he continued, "It's my contention that going to work on Friday in jeans and [a] T-shirt isn't really getting to the nub of the issue." So true. The laugh was a bonus. Everything would have been fine if he didn't get any because, like Esther Perel, he was going for levity, not laughter.

Find levity in the cold, hard truth.

A (Somewhat) Secret Disclosure

Conversational asides are a great way to inject some levity into your presentations. You know I use quotations once in a while in my talks. Sometimes I will add a conversational aside to keep the circuit closed. For example, when speaking about Shrinking the Wall, I might reference the "secret to being a bore" quote by French philosopher Voltaire you read in that chapter and then say quietly to someone close by, "By the way, I've never read Voltaire and I don't want to pretend that I have. I just love that quote!" I know the mic will pick up the aside so others in the room can hear in the hope they will get a rise from it, which they often do.

It's helpful to prepare these asides in advance, and you need to deliver them as in-the-room ad libs for them to work.

Prepare and share a quiet aside—for all to hear.

I'm just preparing my impromptu remarks.

ATTRIBUTED TO SIR WINSTON CHURCHILL

Anchor Your Feet

You may be excited to integrate movement into your talk because you have seen an inspiring speaker work the stage at a conference or your place of worship. My advice? Not so fast. Movement is not a good use of your attention and energy. It offers limited upside and considerable downside. You will get far greater return on the focus and effort you place on the circuit-closing skills outlined in this chapter (eye contact, speaking in a conversational tone, adding animation, and pausing) than you will on movement.

Once you have nailed these high-return habits, *then* you can integrate some purposeful movement into your repertoire. In the interim, stand still. As with so many things, this is easy to say and hard to do. Sir Ken Robinson had a hard time moving because of his polio, yet standing in one spot didn't hurt his extraordinary ability to command the room.

Many people spill their energy through extraneous movement. Imagine you have a large spring inside your torso. When you are under pressure it is as though the spring gets wound and compressed tightly. The spring wants to unwind to release the energy, and the energy release often comes through your feet—you will find yourself shifting your weight from foot to foot, drifting around in front of the audience, or pacing like a caged tiger at the zoo. Most people are unaware of their ineffective movement because it is happening subconsciously.

Try to override this tendency to move, and anchor your presence by standing still. The act of standing is easy if it's the only thing you're doing. As soon as you add in the need to think about your content and deliver it with eye contact, animation, and gravitas, your feet often become unmoored. As you begin to drift, your presence shrinks.

To train yourself to stay in place, try standing on flip chart paper or tinfoil, as it will give you real-time crinkly feedback if you're starting to shift your weight. Your goal is to keep your lower torso quiet to keep the paper under your feet silent. If you stand with your feet a little bit more than shoulder width apart it will be harder for you to shift your weight from foot to foot. Stand up and give it a go right now.

**I can tell whether a person
can play just by the way he stands.**
ATTRIBUTED TO MILES DAVIS

"Oh, but I like to stand behind a lectern because it helps me stand still," I often hear. Unless you are in court or delivering the State of the Union address, lose the training wheels and remove the physical barrier between you and your audience. While it might make you feel more comfortable, it will impede your ability to connect with your audience.

If you remove the lectern, it will also reduce the likelihood you'll read from notes. When conference organizers say they want to do TED-style talks, they're referring to substance and style: insightful, story-driven content delivered in the room, without a lectern.

Once you have firmly grounded your presence, try to remain in place for at least thirty seconds, particularly at the beginning of your talk. When you have built muscle memory for the more high-return habits, here are some ways to start integrating some movement.

Start small by moving your feet slightly, to allow you to square up your presence, and reinforce your eye contact to a different part of the room. Repeat periodically. Research reinforces that when you orient your torso toward those you are addressing, you communicate a more positive attitude toward them.[14] You can use this approach when seated in swivel chairs around a boardroom table too.

Then add some purposeful movement. Walk back to point at a specific word or image on the screen (but don't talk to the screen when you're pointing at it) and return to the front of the stage or close to the boardroom table to elaborate on the point. Sure, you can make one or two points while standing back beside the screen, but don't get stranded there for long stretches of time.

You could also move to delineate perspectives. You could stand on one side to outline the advantages of using Python programming language and then walk a few paces to the other side where you will set out the disadvantages. When speaking on a larger stage, you can also move to spend time with different sections of the audience. Stand still as you elaborate, to ground your presence.

When you have important and emotive points to make, try to deliver them closer to your audience. Research has shown that communicators who adopt close proximity are perceived as more persuasive and dominant.[15] Anchor your feet to solidify the import of the point as you deliver it.

Aim to stand still for at least 90 percent of your talk. Imagine you're standing on the circular TED carpet and you can't step off it—this will minimize the tendency you may have to drift around like an unloved floaty toy in a bathtub.

Stand still for most of your talk. After you've nailed the rest of the circuit-closing habits, then add some purposeful movement into your repertoire.

6

CAPITALIZE ON QUESTIONS

Four Letters Cratered a Campaign

The Guardian described it as "one of the most humiliating debate performances in recent US political history."[1] It was November 9, 2011, and Governor Rick Perry began to answer a question in a national debate to determine the Republican Party's nominee for president.

"There are three agencies of government when I get there that are gone: commerce, education, and, and the, what's the third one? Let's see..." and the governor stalled. Earlier in the race, he had been leading in the polls with 30 percent.[2] As he began to lose his grip on his answer, he somehow managed to momentarily maintain his telegenic presence, bolstered by his Ken doll brown hair, black suit, starched white shirt, and uniform-completing red power tie.

He playfully bantered with some of the other candidates who were throwing him unhelpful bones like, "The EPA?" to which he and everyone laughed. The laughter quickly became the awkward kind as everyone sensed they were on the cusp of a fumble that could turn into a face plant.

"Seriously? You can't name the third?" said the moderator, grabbing a hold of Perry, who was hoping the moment would slip.

"The third agency of government I would do away with, um, the um, commerce, and let's see..." He paused and drew his jaw back as though it was blocking his view of his notes. He turned them over, hoping for the answer to reveal itself. It wasn't there. "Let's see... I can't. The third one, I can't. Sorry," he offered, nodding his head to the side like he was unblocking a drop of water in his ear. Then he turned to the candidate on his right and said, "Oops."

Perry's debate performance cratered his campaign—a campaign where he was a contender poised to give Mitt Romney and Herman Cain a run for their money. One minute he was a star candidate with sights set on the White House, and one "Oops" later he was headed toward *Dancing with the Stars*.

To say that Q&A can be perilous is not an understatement for Perry. For the rest of us, the consequences aren't typically as dire. In fact, Q&A can be an opportunity to shine as you nimbly respond to queries, demonstrate your command of your expertise, and engender confidence in your audience.

Warren Buffett explicitly asks for tough questions during Q&A, saying, "I prefer fastballs." As hard as they're thrown, he swats them away like softballs. To see him quote Japanese interest rates twelve years prior, to three decimal places, in response to a question is remarkable.

Computers are useless. They can only give you the answers.

PABLO PICASSO

To Respond or Not to Respond

Often you can choose how much Q&A, if any, you'll do. Here are some guidelines to help you decide.

As a general rule, the larger the audience, the less useful Q&A is. Many thoughtful people are less inclined to ask questions in front of a big crowd; they've worked hard to cultivate their intellect, and they're fearful of saying something that's not polished. Those remaining are often grandstanders, bloviators, or ax-grinders, who don't tend to make for good Q&A. I saw Fareed Zakaria speak to a thousand professionals, which he did brilliantly, before he took some questions. Everyone's time would have been better spent if he had extended his keynote because the questions limited him.

If you can confidently achieve your objectives without a Q&A session and you see some risk of opening the floor, then don't have one. Q&As are especially risky if the topic is new to you and you're concerned you won't have the answers. You've worked hard to prep your outbound remarks, but you can't control the inbound questions, so you may choose to avoid them.

Conversely, if the likelihood of you achieving your objectives improves with Q&A, go for it. If you're advancing a contentious position that requires enlisting the support of the audience, failure to let them speak and challenge you will likely hinder your cause. Open up and let them ask. This will also open up an opportunity for spontaneity where you're in the room having a lively exchange with your audience.

Consider the trade-offs before deciding to open the floor to questions.

Risk Management Meets Tough Questions

The prospect of being asked tough questions stresses out many speakers. While you can't eliminate the possibility of tough questions, you can reduce the likelihood of them arising before you get to the Q&A session.

Ensure your content is relevant, clear, and compelling. If it isn't, the audience may become more impatient and ratchet up the intensity of their queries. In other words, follow the process: Shrink the Wall, create an Idea Quiver, build Power Messages.

Speak to engender confidence. Weak delivery creates uncertainty, and audiences may be more inclined to challenge and test you. Don't let circling sharks smell blood. Close the Circuit.

Anticipate questions you could be asked and prep your answers. Even if you don't get asked those questions, you'll be more confident walking into the room knowing you have prepared for them, and it will show. Sometimes you can canvas those who know members of the audience or people similar to them and ask, "What would be the toughest questions they could ask me about my topic?"

We learned from astronaut and Top 100 speaker Chris Hadfield that NASA knows the importance of anticipating and practicing countless disaster scenarios.[3] This training helped him keep his cool when he lost his vision during a spacewalk. His eyes filled with so much goop he couldn't see for minutes. With a lot of composure, patience, and blinking, he cleared his eyes and completed his walk. He later discovered some of the anti-fog mixture from his helmet had got in his eyes. Now they use No More Tears to clean visors.

Reduce Q&A risk by following the prep process and practice so you can handle goop-in-the-eye tough questions.

Q&A Composure

Once you're in Q&A, there are a number of tactics that help you shine, starting with listening to the end of the question. A young litigator took questions after he presented to his peers in a health law group at a firm offsite in Kingston. Before he heard the end of the first question, he turned around and walked away from the questioner with an I-know-what-you're-going-to-say-and-I-already-know-my-response nod. He came off as arrogant and rude. Conversely, practiced politicians tend to be very good at waiting until the end of the question before they signal they are ready to respond, even if it's a question they receive frequently. People want to be heard.

Consider if the question is sitting atop of another deeper concern—are they asking about tariffs or are they really asking about your position on free markets?

After you've listened, give yourself space to think. You have more time to reflect than you likely are giving yourself. As long as you don't look uncomfortable, you can take more time to consider before you respond. Don't walk backward and look skyward and say, "Ummm" as you think. Show composure: stand still, maintain eye contact or look at your notes—even if the answer is not there—and allow for some silence.

If you don't understand the question, ask to have it rephrased. Or rephrase it yourself, and ask the questioner to confirm that's what they meant. This shows you're listening and, hopefully, get it.

Consider providing structured answers, for example, "A few things: First [pause] ... Second [pause] ..." You can add a third part if you want. This approach creates hidden pauses so you can think. It also encourages clarity, concision, and conviction, all of which engender confidence. Don't box yourself in by stating how many parts of your answer there will be unless you're certain you will remember them all. Had Governor Perry begun his response by simply saying, "There are a few agencies of government that are gone when I get there: First, commerce...," he could have ended his answer after two and avoided the end of his candidacy.

Listen to the whole question, create time to think by pausing and paraphrasing, and provide structured responses where possible.

Uh-Oh, I Don't Know

A source of Q&A anxiety is the fear of being stumped. There are a range of strategies to help you keep cool and respond when your first thoughts are coming up short.

In some cases, you might ask, "Tell me a little more about why you are asking to give me some context." When they elaborate, you may find you have something helpful to say.

Another option is to redirect the question to someone else in the room. I know this strategy is used at weekly all-hands meetings at a tech giant in Silicon Valley, where the CEO takes questions and frequently redirects the question to other leaders attending. If you do this, it's helpful to give the person a couple of seconds notice; for example, "I'm going to turn it over to Chris to respond. Before I do, here's my two cents..."

Sometimes you can redirect the question back to the audience: "Collectively, we have a lot of experience in the room. Have any of you dealt with this situation, and if so, what's worked or not worked?" One of my clients who is new to presenting on a topic uses this approach effectively. You become the facilitator to the answer and can think while others are chiming in. If you think you might have something to contribute, you could say, "I've got one or two thoughts on this. Before

I share them, let's go to the audience to see what they think or have found to work, or not." If you have expertise but not enough context to provide a specific answer, you could qualify and then go to first principles. For example, "I would need to know more about the situation you are in, but here are the elements I would use to help determine what's the best approach."

One of the most common approaches is to simply say you don't know. Don't make a big deal of not knowing. Offer to investigate and follow up. If you have asked them to tell you more about why they are asking, as suggested above, you'll regain some control and their response can guide your research, so you can ultimately provide a better response. Senator Obama was campaigning in May 2008 when he was asked about his position on cleaning up the nuclear waste site in Hanford, Washington, where scientists helped to create the atomic bomb.

"Here's something that you will rarely hear from a politician, and that is that I'm not familiar with the Hanford site, so I don't know exactly what's going on there," Obama said as he calmly walked toward the questioner. "Now, having said that, I promise you I'll learn about it by the time I leave here on the ride back to the airport."[4]

Obama had an escape hatch, and you likely have one too. As one of my senior clients, Terri, said to some of her juniors before they gave a talk, "There's very little that can't be undone later. I've said more than once before, 'You know, I've thought about what I said earlier, and it strikes me it wasn't the most thoughtful response. Here's what I think will be more helpful...'"

If you're stumped, redirect the question to others, provide general guidance, or offer to investigate and report back later.

Disarming and Defusing Sticky Situations

The more you speak, the more you will encounter sticky situations that can make your temperature rise. Having a few tactics at the ready can help disarm a situation quickly.

To manage grandstanders, consider pre-emptively acknowledging their presence—in a complimentary way—early in your remarks. This recognition may reduce their need to chest-puff. I've seen the same retired justice in an audience in two separate talks. In the first, he pontificated during the Q&A for minutes without ever posing a question. In the second, the speaker acknowledged he was in the audience and had considerable experience before saying, "So, Justice, I may call on you to help me with some questions later on." The justice nodded and looked as though the teacher had just announced he'd got the top grade. He didn't say a word during the question period.

Have a light-hearted comment at hand to wind down an exchange with a long-winded audience member, such as, "You and I should have a breakout discussion at the pub tonight. While we're here, let's give others a chance to jump in." And with that, turn away and look to a different part of the room, and call for the next question.

Show that you've heard them. Like most of us, bloviators and ax-grinders want public validation. Even if you disagree with them, you can let them know you've heard them: "Sounds like you are committed to [insert point], and I understand why [reflect back part of their rationale]. I get it. Others have a different perspective. Let's give them a chance to outline theirs…" Or, "Here's another way of looking at it…"

To turn down the emotional temperature with a hostile questioner, try to disentangle the facts from how they have interpreted and evaluated those facts: "As I heard from you, the person arrived five minutes late to the meeting. You think this shows a lack of organization and respect. Is that right?" Try to discuss the facts first and get agreement on those *before* discussing their interpretation of the facts. Once you've clarified the facts, you could also ask them for other possible interpretations. In many cases, it's helpful to check in and ask if you answered the question.

Separate facts from interpretations to encourage a more productive and respectful exchange.

Tactics to Be Used in Moderation

You can sparingly say, "That's a great question." This will give you a beat to think. But if you begin every response using it, then you will seem disingenuous and it will appear as though you are buying time. Not all questions are great, so don't say they are.

Similarly, don't repeat back every question unless you are doing it because you know some people in the audience didn't hear it. Infrequently, you can repeat it back to set up the emphasis of your answer. This is what politician Stacey Abrams did to great effect in a town hall when asked about regulating big tech companies. "The question is, 'Do I believe that there should be a regulatory scheme that looks at the evolution of essentially an entirely new economy in America?' Yes." After the audience applauded—in Seattle no less—she completed her answer.[5]

Finally, if you plan to answer the question you wish they'd asked instead of the one that was actually asked, you are on slippery terrain. By all means, answer the initial question and then go beyond to cover something else that's related and important, but don't ignore the question.

Only repeat questions to confirm you've understood a complex or unclear question or if others in the room didn't hear it.

If you still have questions about questions, you may be interested to expand your research into media training, where you can learn strategies to address questions with a false premise or false choice and more. (Hint: Don't repeat or agree with the premise.) The approaches in this chapter are more than sufficient to prep most people for most non-media Q&A.

If you know your stuff, you will shine in Q&A. As a bonus, anticipating how you'll respond to tricky questions before you walk into the room will boost your confidence, even if the tricky ones don't get asked.

7

COMPOUND YOUR CONFIDENCE

THE HEAD OF a major cosmetics company said, "We don't sell cosmetics. We sell hope." In that vein, we don't sell presentation coaching, we sell confidence. At some point you will feel anxious about speaking, whether it's at a weekly meeting with colleagues or an annual general meeting, and you'll want to build your confidence.

A Nervous Anchor

"I need to speak to a group of 800 in Calgary in ten days and I'm nervous," was the simple briefing I was given. The fact that someone was nervous before speaking wasn't surprising, but that *this* person was nervous was. Bruce Sellery is a journalist who had just returned from New York City, where he'd spent years as a TV anchor for a business news show speaking to a massive audience every day. He'd just spoken at a chamber of commerce, and people in the audience wrote him to tell him how much they'd enjoyed his talk.

If a seasoned, smart, and funny journalist and accomplished speaker can experience nerves, we all can. Speaking anxiety is the most commonly cited social fear, whether it's speaking in public or speaking up in a meeting or class.[1]

After a content strategy session, I asked, "How are you feeling now?" Sellery said, "Great. I need to tweak a few things, which I can do on the plane. But great, nerves are gone." Once his content was ready, he knew he could deliver it with confidence.

Let's explore some strategies to manage anxiety that work for everyone, whether you're a professional speaker like Sellery or just a professional who needs to speak.

Return on Rehearsal

The corporate finance group at one of the Big Four did an analysis to figure out what they should do to increase their success when pitching for new business. Top of the list was doing a team rehearsal. Makes sense. It's a forcing function: in order to rehearse, you need to be prepared. Rehearsal reveals who is and who isn't ready. Better to drive yourself and your team to prepare earlier than hope for things to magically come together for the first time in front of the client.

No, you're not better when you wing it. You may think you're better, but you're either blissfully ignorant, in denial, or got lucky when serendipity struck one time.

"I hate rehearsing, but I know it makes for a better session," one of my clients said. "It's like eating spinach. It makes you stronger. And it's time better spent than tinkering with slides." Aye aye, Popeye.

Pros rehearse and amateurs don't, whether it's sports, music, or business. Watch the Netflix documentary *Gaga: Five Foot Two*, and you'll see just how hard she rehearses, even as an established pop star.

Here are nine steps to get you ready to rock the room:

1 If you have a script, use it as a starting point. Read it out loud while sitting down. Rehearsing out loud is five times more powerful than practicing in your head.

2 Then bold the gold—the key phrases that could serve as helpful prompts. Practice delivering the talk using only the bolded phrases as prompts. Give yourself permission to say it differently than you'd initially scripted, as this will allow you to be in the room and speak conversationally. You can do this sitting down.

3 Repeat Step 2 while standing up.

4 Repeat, but now focusing on your delivery: Pause to reference your notes; practice making eye contact for three to five seconds per person; gesticulate to delineate points...

5 Get constructive feedback from a friend or a colleague whom you trust. This is a great way to hop off the worry wagon and build your confidence. Constructive feedback has been shown to be more helpful than positive feedback when it is focused on the most important areas to improve.[2] Ask for specific suggestions that you can act on. Your presentation will get better, and you'll be able to rein in counterproductive thoughts in your imagination.

6 Record your rehearsal. It helps you see what others have described. Even if you understand the feedback on a rational level, the video will help you appreciate it more viscerally. While you may not enjoy watching yourself on video—most don't—you may be positively surprised: many

say, "It was better than I thought," after reviewing their baseline performance. They are often even struck when they see in subsequent clips how small improvements have made a big difference to their effectiveness, which builds their confidence.

7   Rehearse at the venue, if possible, with all the technology you'll be using in your talk: mic, lighting, slides, comfort monitor, and presentation remote. Knowing the equipment works inspires confidence. It's amazing how often some troubleshooting is required before a speaking engagement—better to have the kinks ironed out in advance. Be friendly with and respectful of the AV support team, and don't be afraid to ask them to make adjustments to help you, such as changing the comfort monitor position or the formatting of your notes on it.

8   On presentation day, show up early to do a sound check and make sure everything works. And drink warm or room-temperature water, as cold water will tighten your vocal cords. Oh, and learn how to operate the mute on your microphone—best to doublecheck you're muted before going into the restroom and avoid the embarrassment like that created by Alec Baldwin's character in *30 Rock*.[3]

9   Rehearse your intro and closing more than the core of your talk. Chances are, you are more comfortable talking about the middle, so you'll have more nerves at the beginning. Practicing the top and tail will help you start and finish strong.

Rehearse. It makes you stronger.

Thankfully, perseverance is a great substitute for talent.

STEVE MARTIN

Transparency Is an Illusion

You might believe your nerves are 100 percent transparent. They're not. There is a gap between how nervous you feel and how nervous you look and sound. While you may sense that your hands are shaking, your voice is about to crack, and your palms are sweating, the audience won't notice most, if any, of that.[4]

After speaking, many people will tell me and the rest of their team they felt incredibly nervous. I ask them to rate how nervous they felt by writing a number between 1 and 10 (1 = confident, 10 = the cusp of a coronary). Then I ask members of the audience to assess the speaker on the same scale. Every single time I have done this, the speaker self-assesses at a higher level than the audience's assessment—typically double.

Try recording yourself while speaking. Before reviewing the footage, assess how nervous you felt. Then watch the playback and assess how nervous you seemed. When you recognize that you don't appear to be as nervous as you feel, your anxiety will go down and your performance will improve. This is a much better spot to be in than being stuck in the vicious circle: worried people feel nervous, which makes them more nervous.

Remind yourself that your nerves aren't transparent.

The Bootcamp Boost

Training works. Many studies have shown that it improves your effectiveness and confidence. In one, a group of students were assessed on their speaking s.. .ıs and confidence before they received instruction, which included hands-on practice and feedback. After the training, the students were reassessed, and all their scores had improved significantly—both based on skill development and self-confidence.[5]

	Pre-training assessment (percent of target behavior)	Post-training assessment (percent of target behavior)
Gestures	12%	81%
Eye contact	4%	98%
Speaking behaviors including position on stage, thanking host, greeting audience, introducing topic, asking for questions	13%	100%
Overall rating (7 is very good, 1 is very bad)	2.2	5.5
How confident were you when giving your talk? (7 is very confident, 1 is very unconfident)	3.6	5.9

SOURCE: Stephen B. Fawcett and L. Keith Miller, "Training Public-Speaking Behavior: An Experimental Analysis and Social Validation," *Journal of Applied Behavior Analysis* 8, no. 2 (1975): 125–35.

I've seen the same pattern of improvement over the decades I've been leading intensive speaker-training programs.

Get some training and enjoy the confidence boost.

Focus Outwardly

Like it or not, when you speak, you're being evaluated—formally or informally. When you know you are going to be evaluated, your anxiety goes up. Highly anxious speakers have been shown to make less eye contact and more nervous gestures and to look at their notes more frequently than those who aren't.[6]

You're being evaluated on your content, too. When an audience appears interested in your remarks, your anxiety goes down—even if they look like they're negatively reacting to the material![7] To help you be judged as favorably as possible on content and delivery, you know what to do: Shrink the Wall, create an Idea Quiver, build Power Messages, and Close the Circuit!

The act of preparing in this way will also shift your attention from what could be a negative self-focus ("I'm worried I'll sound like an idiot") to a positive other-focus ("How can I help my audience?"). It's not about you, it's about them—the audience. Put your attention on them, and your anxiety will go down.

When you are speaking, think about it as delivering to one person at a time, rather than speaking to a large group. You'll recall I recommend you make eye contact for three to five seconds per person to strengthen your connection and presence. It will also help you make a series of micro, one-on-one presentations that feel more personal and less intimidating. This is Simon Sinek's approach.

"If you notice, I've learned to leverage what I have. So, it makes me a much better public speaker because I am an introvert, because I don't like holding court. It freaks me out. But I like talking to individuals," Sinek says. "So, you'll notice when I speak, I'm talking to you." He points and looks at one person, "and then I talk to you," he points and looks at another person, "and then talk to you," he points and looks at another. "[This] actually helps me connect with an audience much better."[8]

If you repeatedly follow the same prep process and consistently get good results, you will start to have confidence in the process itself. Next time you follow it, you will expect a positive outcome, which will build your confidence.

The sooner you prepare, the sooner your anxiety goes down and your confidence goes up. You don't have to spend more time preparing, just start Shrinking the Wall sooner.

Prepare to be other-focused and deliver to one person at a time.

The Pursuit of Peace

Your anxiety levels are likely to rise when you have to speak to a lot of people, negative people, or other experts in your topic.[9] Try to build your confidence by speaking to the opposite: small groups of friendly people who are not experts.

When I was in my twenties, I participated in Toastmasters for three years because it gave me a chance to practice public speaking with people who were positive and supportive. It's a great, affordable organization. For those who are time-starved, want to improve quickly, and have funds to invest, there are more efficient ways to grow, such as intensive programs led by experts.

"I used to start getting nervous after Labor Day before an annual address I'd give every December to hundreds, including members of the exec committee," a client told me. I challenged him to take incremental risks when speaking to small audiences of junior professionals, which he did frequently. "Now I don't get nervous until two weeks before the event—that's three months of welcome peace," he reported.

Speak to small, supportive audiences to build confidence for the intimidating ones.

Confidence for Sunday

Pro golf tournaments are four days of high pressure with big dollars on the line and millions of people watching. All this pressure comes to a head on Sunday, when the tourney concludes. What's the simplest thing the pros do that you can adopt? Practice. Practice at the driving range and practice in matches. This cumulative practice builds confidence. As Tiger Woods says, "I just think there's a certain calmness that comes with being able to say with honesty that I've done this before. That's the calmness I feel down the stretch."[10]

To make the most of your practice, focus on one thing at a time when there is low pressure. Golfers call it a "swing thought": focus on only one thought when you swing. Speakers can do the same. You might focus solely on eye contact during routine, round-table meetings. Don't worry about the rest of the delivery skills for a set period of time, say a week. Then shift your attention to another delivery skill such as pausing. Practice pausing when you are delegating tasks, for example. If you practice one thing at a time, when there is little or no pressure, you will build a habit. As you layer a new habit on another new habit, they will compound in their power.

If you try to focus on too many things concurrently, you will get tangled up and feel like you are trying to rub your belly, pat your head, and jump up and down on one foot as you say the alphabet backward. That's a recipe for frustration and eroding your confidence. Focus on one thing and make it a habit.

Deliberately practice one thing at a time to build high-value habits.

You can't be that kid standing at the top of the waterslide, overthinking it. You have to go down the chute.

TINA FEY

Confidence Begets Confidence

There was a reality TV competition for filmmakers a few years ago produced by Steven Spielberg, Mark Burnett, and David Goffin. The show, *On the Lot,* featured weekly elimination challenges where contestants vied to win a million-dollar development deal with DreamWorks.

Andrew Hunt, a thirty-one-year-old participant, pitched to a panel of accomplished Hollywood directors. "My logline is a priest who finds the girl of his dreams right before he gets ordained," Hunt began. In the next ninety seconds, the beanie-wearing, bespectacled contestant told a story about Charlie Potts, a priest who's on track to be the next big bishop. Potts develops a relationship with a pilot, Alex, who flies in supplies to his mission in South America. "She's wild, she's crazy, she's everything he's not. She's teaching him how to do things like how to dance for the first time, how to take shots of tequila."

Potts is starting to fall in love with Alex when a flood rips through the village where they're staying. After working frantically to get people to higher ground, the pair gets separated. The next day the rain stops. Potts searches desperately to find the pilot and finally does.

"On the roof, he sees Alex. She's passed out or she's dead. He's looking up saying, 'I've never asked you for anything, but I'm asking you for one thing right now.'" Hunt paused to let the tension build. "Finally, she coughs up water. She's alive." He paused again before setting the next scene.

"Now we're in Boston, Massachusetts, in a huge church." When he said "huge," Hunt shoved his hands out wide before finishing, "and we see Charlie standing there about ready to get ordained. But then we pull back to see it's a wedding. We're out."

"Can you give my next pitch to the studio?" asked one judge immediately afterwards. Another judge said, "Let's give him the money. That's how great your pitch was; it made me take my wallet out." Another piled on, "You inspire confidence by being so confident." As Hunt turned to walk out the door, the most senior judge said under his breath, "Andrew Hunt, very good . . ."

Systematically build your confidence so you can engender confidence in others.

CONCLUSION
MOVING MILLIONS

IMAGINE PEOPLE muttering your name under their breath after your next talk because they are so impressed. The chances of this happening to you are a lot higher than you may think. There are a lot of mediocre speakers out there, and it doesn't take a lot to stand out. All it takes is doing a few things differently and better. When you do, you will change the trajectory of your career and the impact you will make. Speaking is the enabling skill at the center of so many improbable success stories.

It was for Barack Obama, when he spoke at the Democratic National Convention, where he moved the room and was elevated to the national stage. He built on this momentum and went on to move millions—even billions—through his speaking and governing.

It was for Brené Brown, when she climbed on stage in Houston and moved the room. She built on this momentum and has done extraordinary work moving millions through her writing, speaking, and programs. Ten years later, guess who she landed as a guest on her leadership podcast? The forty-fourth president of the United States—not an opportunity given to any other professors of social work, but an opportunity she earned. During their conversation, Obama even referenced the inflection point in his career: "I arrived on the national scene based on my convention speech in Boston in 2004."[1]

It was for Lin-Manuel Miranda, when he convinced an initial group of investors to put $12.5 million into *Hamilton*—far from an easy pitch. After his breakout success, the Obamas introduced Miranda at the Tony Awards, where they explained they had met years before when Miranda had performed at the White House. The Obamas had laughed when Miranda had told them he planned to teach civics through rap in a musical. At the Tonys, they admitted the joke was on them.

When Miranda finished the rousing number "My Shot" in the show's title role, he did it with power. Wearing his waistcoat and high leather boots, he marched forward with his coattails fluttering behind. As he arrived downstage close to the audience, he planted his feet, then finished with the final line—"Not throwin' away my shot"—thrusting his arm into the air as he hit the final beat of the number on the word "shot."

Miranda moved millions in his audiences. *Hamilton* has generated over $1 billion in revenue.[2] It's safe to say Miranda made his shot. With firmly planted feet, now it's time for you to make yours.

ACKNOWLEDGMENTS

> There is no such thing as a self-made man. You will
> reach your goals only with the help of others.
>
> GEORGE SHINN, FORMER OWNER OF THE NEW ORLEANS HORNETS

IN MARCH OF 2020, when COVID-19 started to race around the world, my calendar quickly emptied of commitments as my clients scrambled to shift their work online and shore up their businesses. When I spoke with my dear friend Jeff Davis shortly after March Break, he said, "You should write your book now." Great idea, but I doubted myself.

One of my many shortcomings is I'm often unable to finish projects that take more than a couple of months to complete. I get distracted by other opportunities that promise faster dopamine hits. The odds of me publishing a book were long. Were it not for the structure and support of the terrific team at Page Two, this book would remain a decades-old dream with a fifty-seven-word subtitle.

I'm grateful to Page Two cofounder Jesse Finkelstein for her positive spirit and sage counsel throughout this process.

My editor, Scott Steedman, continually nudged me in the right direction and built my confidence. Details matter, and Jenny Govier's attention to them is remarkable and her copyediting strengthened the book. Rony Ganon's deft project management helped me focus on the right thing at the right time. Peter Cocking, Taysia Louie, and Fiona Lee produced a stunning array of creative cover designs and I'm delighted with where we landed.

Madeleine Cohen pored through the library stacks at U of T to find and summarize more research than I could read in a year—if I could find it at all.

I've lost track of the number of times my morning runs over the past year with John Warrillow were spent tapping his wisdom as an author. I slowed him down during our runs and he sped up my writing: one of his tips alone helped me write the book in half the time it would have taken otherwise.

I'm thankful for my clients. For decades they have given me their trust and allowed me to refine my approach as a coach. I am indebted to them for their willingness to share their stories to bring the ideas on these pages alive.

My high school English teacher, Mr. Morrow, taught me it was possible to improve as a writer. I'm still working on it. Professor Smallbridge taught me writing could be fun. I'm still working on it.

My parents showed me it's possible to make things happen if we get at it and work hard. Their example is a gift to my sister and me.

My wife, Clara, shows me every day that the most powerful way to move a room is with love. Thank you for yours.

NOTES

Introduction: Speaking Is a Force Multiplier

1 Brené Brown, "The Power of Vulnerability," TED, June 2010, ted.com/ talks/brene_brown_the_power_of_vulnerability.

2 Brené Brown, "Listening to Shame," TED, March 2012, ted.com/talks/ brene_brown_listening_to_shame.

3 Combined views of "The Power of Vulnerability" on TED.com (ted.com/ talks/brene_brown_the_power_of_vulnerability) and YouTube (youtube. com/watch?v=iCvmsMzlF70) as of January 2021.

4 "About," on Brené Brown's official website, brenebrown.com/about/ brenebrown.com/about.

5 Maria Aspan, "How This Leadership Researcher Became the Secret Weapon for Oprah, Pixar, IBM, and Melinda Gates," *Inc.*, October 2018, inc.com/magazine/201810/maria-aspan/brene-brown-leadership-consultant-research.html.

6 Harry Beckwith, *The Invisible Touch: The Four Keys to Modern Marketing* (New York: Warner Books, 2000), 195.

Chapter 1: Shrink the Wall

1 "Encarta," Wikipedia, en.wikipedia.org/wiki/Encarta.

2 Ben White, "Merrill Lynch to Pay Fine, Tighten Rules on Analysts," *Washington Post*, May 22, 2002, washingtonpost.com/archive/politics/ 2002/05/22/merrill-lynch-to-pay-fine-tighten-rules-on-analysts/ 27fc5858-3597-465d-9402-2bd60e2a2366.

3 Natasha Scripture, "What Is the TED Prize (and How Can You Win Next Year's)?" *TED Blog*, March 26, 2014, blog.ted.com/what-is-the-ted-prize-and-how-can-you-win-next-years.

Chapter 2: Create an Idea Quiver

1   "Steve Jobs Introduces iPhone in 2007," posted by John Schroter, YouTube, October 9, 2011, youtu.be/MnrJzXM7a6o.

2   Julian Treasure, "5 Ways to Listen Better," TED, July 2011, ted.com/talks/julian_treasure_5_ways_to_listen_better.

3   Malika Favre, *The Operating Theatre*, illustration, *New Yorker* cover, April 3, 2017, newyorker.com/magazine/2017/04/03.

4   Françoise Mouly, "Cover Story: Malika Favre's *Operating Theatre*," *New Yorker*, March 23, 2017, newyorker.com/culture/culture-desk/cover-story-2017-04-03.

5   Megan Ogilvie, "The Power of Female Surgeons Unmasked around the World Thanks to a Magazine Cover," *Toronto Star*, April 20, 2017, thestar.com/news/canada/2017/04/20/the-power-of-female-surgeons-unmasked-around-the-world-thanks-to-a-magazine-cover.html?rf.

Chapter 3: Add Power Messages

1   Barack Obama, 2015 State of the Union Address, January 12, 2016, Obama White House Archives, obamawhitehouse.archives.gov/state-of-the-union-2015.

2   Corey Robin, "Ronald Reagan's Balcony Heroes," *Harvard University Press Blog*, February 2, 2018, harvardpress.typepad.com/hup_publicity/2018/02/ronald-reagan-heroes-in-the-balcony-daniel-rodgers.html.

3   Ronald Reagan, Address before a Joint Session of the Congress Reporting on the State of the Union, January 26, 1982, American Presidency Project, presidency.ucsb.edu/node/245636.

4   "What Is the Growth Share Matrix?" Boston Consulting Group, bcg.com/en-ca/about/our-history/growth-share-matrix.

5   Tiffany Hsu and Sapna Maheshwari, "'Thumb-Stopping,' 'Humaning,' 'B4H': The Strange Language of Modern Marketing," *New York Times*, November 25, 2020, nytimes.com/2020/11/25/business/media/thumb-stopping-humaning-b4h-the-strange-language-of-modern-marketing.html.

6   Ray Dalio, "How the Economic Machine Works," YouTube, September 22, 2013, youtube.com/watch?v=PHe0bXAIuko.

7   "Facebook COO Sheryl Sandberg's First Sit-Down with Ellen," *The Ellen Show*, YouTube, April 24, 2017, youtu.be/_TFVTPOQ1Sc?t=174.

8   Don Lindsay, email message to author, January 2, 2021.

9   Paul J. Zak, "Why Your Brain Loves Good Storytelling," *Harvard Business Review*, October 28, 2014, hbr.org/2014/10/why-your-brain-loves-good-storytelling.

10 Martha Hamilton and Mitch Weiss, *Children Tell Stories: Teaching and Using Storytelling in the Classroom* (Katonah, NY: Richard C. Owen Publishers, 2005), 206.

11 Don Hewitt, *Tell Me a Story: Fifty Years and 60 Minutes in Television* (New York: Public Affairs, 2001), 1.

12 Steven Goff, "Megan Rapinoe vs. Lucy Bronze in a World Cup Semifinal Is a Star-Power Matchup Like No Other," *Washington Post*, June 30, 2019, washingtonpost.com/sports/2019/06/30/megan-rapinoe-vs-lucy-bronze-world-cup-semifinal-is-star-power-matchup-like-no-other.

13 Tehila Kogut and Ilana Ritov, "The 'Identified Victim' Effect: An Identified Group, or Just a Single Individual?" *Journal of Behavioral Decision Making* 18, no. 3 (2005): 157–67, doi.org/10.1002/bdm.492.

14 As cited in Shankar Vedantam, "Why Your Brain Wants to Help One Child in Need—but Not Millions," *Goats and Soda*, NPR, November 5, 2014, npr.org/sections/goatsandsoda/2014/11/05/361433850/why-your-brain-wants-to-help-one-child-in-need-but-not-millions.

15 "Kurt Vonnegut on the Shapes of Stories," posted by David Comberg, YouTube, October 30, 2010, youtu.be/oP3c1h8v2ZQ?t=77.

16 Marc Marschark, "Imagery and Organization in the Recall of Prose," *Journal of Memory and Language* 24, no. 6 (1985): 734–45, doi.org/10.1016/0749-596X(85)90056-7.

17 "The Kitchen and the Experience: Running a Restaurant from 'Both Sides of the Wall,'" *Vanity Fair* New Establishment Summit, October 4, 2017, vanityfair.com/video/watch/the-new-establishment-summit-the-kitchen-and-the-experience-running-a-restaurant-from-both-sides-of-the-wall.

18 Bob Simon, "Conductor Gustavo Dudamel's Musical Mission," *60 Minutes*, May 14, 2010, cbsnews.com/news/conductor-gustavo-dudamels-musical-mission.

19 Warren Buffett, Letter to the Shareholders of Berkshire Hathaway Inc., March 1, 1994, berkshirehathaway.com/letters/1993.html.

20 Jerry Seinfeld, *23 Hours to Kill*, Netflix, 2020.

21 Colin Powell and Joseph E. Persico, *My American Journey* (New York: Ballantine Books, 1995), 102.

22 Interview with Marc Benioff, "'I Know Marketing,'" *Forbes*, January 25, 2007, forbes.com/2007/01/25/salesforce-marketing-benioff-tech-enter-cz_vmb_0125salesforce.html.

23 "Legends Profile: Michael Jordan," NBA.com, nba.com/history/legends/profiles/michael-jordan.

24 Billy Witz, "Spurs' Title Is a Testament to Persistence," *New York Times*, June 17, 2014, nytimes.com/2014/06/17/sports/basketball/spurs-title-is-a-victory-for-persistence.html.

25 "Chaplin Quotations," on the Chaplin family's official website, charlie chaplin.com/en/quotes.

26 Scott Adams, *Dilbert and the Way of the Weasel* (New York: Harper Business, 2003), 38.

27 Dr. Prabhjot Singh quoted in Western Bonime, "Human Centered Design Is Revolutionizing How We Respond to Emergencies Like COVID," *Forbes*, October 25, 2020, forbes.com/sites/westernbonime/ 2020/10/25/human-centered-design-is-revolutionizing-how-we-respond-to-emergencies.

28 "Global Trust in Advertising and Brand Messages," Nielsen, April 10, 2012, nielsen.com/ssa/en/insights/report/2012/global-trust-in-advertising-and-brand-messages-2.

29 Myles Udland, "Fidelity Reviewed Which Investors Did Best and What They Found Was Hilarious," *Business Insider*, September 4, 2014, businessinsider.com/forgetful-investors-performed-best-2014-9.

30 "Warren Buffett: Real Time Net Worth," *Forbes*, forbes.com/profile/ warren-buffett/?sh=754c5ae94639.

31 Barbara Whelehan, "This Is the Average Net Worth by Age," Bankrate, March 13, 2020, bankrate.com/personal-finance/average-net-worth-by-age.

32 See u/hipnosister, "The difference between 1 million . . ." r/woahdude, reddit.com/r/woahdude/comments/343i9n/the_difference_between_ 1_million_and_1_billion_is.

33 Michael Lewis, *Moneyball: The Art of Winning an Unfair Game* (New York: W.W. Norton, 2004), 121.

34 Dan Ariely, "Painful Lessons," web.mit.edu/ariely/www/MIT/Papers/ mypain.pdf.

Chapter 4: Use Enabling Visuals

1 Tom Peters, "Slides," TomPeters.com, tompeters.com/slides.

2 Doris A. Graber, "Say It with Pictures," *Annals of the American Academy of Political and Social Science* 546, no. 1 (1996): 85–96, doi.org/10.1177/ 0002716296546001008.

Chapter 5: Close the Circuit

1 Carolyn P. Atkins, "Perceptions of Speakers with Minimal Eye Contact: Implications for Stutterers," *Journal of Fluency Disorders* 13, no. 6 (1988): 429–36, doi.org/10.1016/0094-730X(88)90011-3.

2   Chris L. Kleinke, "Gaze and Eye Contact: A Research Review," *Psychological Bulletin* 100, no. 1 (1986): 78–100, doi.org/10.1037/0033-2909.100.1.78.

3   David Morgan, "Palin Hand Crib Notes Attract Scrutiny," CBS *News*, February 8, 2010, cbsnews.com/news/palin-hand-crib-notes-attract-scrutiny.

4   Cathy N. Davidson, *Now You See It: How the Brain Science of Attention Will Transform the Way We Live, Work, and Learn* (New York: Viking, 2011), 27.

5   Jon Mooallem, "One Man's Quest to Change the Way We Die," *New York Times*, January 3, 2017, nytimes.com/2017/01/03/magazine/one-mans-quest-to-change-the-way-we-die.html.

6   Donald A. Bligh, *What's the Use of Lectures?* (Exeter, UK: Intellect, 1998), 39.

7   Andrew Rosenberg and Julia Hirschberg, "Charisma Perception from Text and Speech," *Speech Communication* 51, no. 7 (2009): 640–55, doi.org/10.1016/j.specom.2008.11.001.

8   Cynthia McLemore, "The Pragmatic Interpretation of English Intonation: Sorority Speech," dissertation, University of Texas at Austin, 1991.

9   S.E. Brennan and M. Williams, "The Feeling of Another's Knowing: Prosody and Filled Pauses as Cues to Listeners about the Metacognitive States of Speakers," *Journal of Memory and Language* 34, no. 3 (1995): 383–98, doi.org/10.1006/jmla.1995.1017.

10 Mary Roach, "10 Things You Didn't Know about Orgasm," TED, February 2009, ted.com/talks/mary_roach_10_things_you_didn_t_know_about_orgasm.

11 Hannah Summerfelt, Louis Lippman, and Ira E. Hyman Jr., "The Effect of Humor on Memory: Constrained by the Pun," *Journal of General Psychology* 137, no. 4 (2010): 376–94, doi.org/10.1080/00221309.2010.499398.

12 Ranked number 7 as of January 1, 2021, on podcastchart.com.

13 "Scandalous Presidential Affairs in France from Private to Public," Eurochannel, eurochannel.com/en/Scandalous-Presidential-Affairs-in-France.html.

14 Albert Mehrabian, "Nonverbal Communication," *Nebraska Symposium on Motivation, Volume 19*, ed. James K. Cole (Nebraska: University of Nebraska Press, 1971), 111.

15 Judee K. Burgoon, David B. Buller, Jerold L. Hale, and Mark A. de Turck, "Relational Messages Associated With Nonverbal Behaviors," *Human Communication Research* 10, no. 3 (1984): 351–78, doi.org/10.1111/j.1468-2958.1984.tb00023.x.

Chapter 6: Capitalize on Questions

1 Ewen MacAskill, "Rick Perry Forgets Agency He Wants to Scrap in Republican Debate Disaster," *The Guardian*, November 10, 2011, theguardian.com/world/2011/nov/10/rick-perry-forgets-agency-scrap.

2 Don Gonyea, "Perry Has An 'Oops' Moment at GOP's Mich. Debate," NPR.com, November 10, 2011, npr.org/2011/11/10/142198509/perry-stumbles-in-latest-gop-debate.

3 Chris Hadfield, "What I Learned from Going Blind in Space," TED, March 2014, ted.com/talks/chris_hadfield_what_i_learned_from_going_blind_in_space.

4 Matthew Daly, "Stumped by Questioner, Obama Vows to Get Answers to Hanford Cleanup," *Everett Herald*, May 19, 2008, heraldnet.com/news/stumped-by-questioner-obama-vows-to-get-answers-to-hanford-cleanup.

5 Stacey Abrams, "Lead from the Outside," Town Hall Seattle, YouTube, April 26, 2019, youtu.be/IB8jlmxg7ag?t=2839.

Chapter 7: Compound Your Confidence

1 Cybele Garcia-Leal, Alexandre C.B.V. Parente, Cristina M. Del-Ben, et al., "Anxiety and Salivary Cortisol in Symptomatic and Nonsymptomatic Panic Patients and Healthy Volunteers Performing Simulated Public Speaking," *Psychiatry Research* 133, nos. 2-3 (2005): 239-52, doi.org/10.1016/j.psychres.2004.04.010; Ayelet Meron Ruscio, Timothy A. Brown, Wai Tat Chiu, et al., "Social Fears and Social Phobia in the USA: Results from the National Comorbidity Survey Replication," *Psychological Medicine* 38, no. 17 (2008): 15-28, dx.doi.org/10.1017%2FS0033291707001699.

2 Graham D. Bodie, "A Racing Heart, Rattling Knees, and Ruminative Thoughts: Defining, Explaining, and Treating Public Speaking Anxiety," *Communication Education* 59, no. 1 (2010): 70-105, doi.org/10.1080/03634520903443849.

3 "Jack's Microphone Mishap—*30 Rock*," posted by 30 Rock Official, YouTube, September 26, 2017, youtube.com/watch?v=6f0SgzpEEQU.

4 Kenneth Savitsky and Thomas Gilovich, "The Illusion of Transparency and the Alleviation of Speech Anxiety," *Journal of Experimental Social Psychology* 39, no. 6 (2003): 618-25, doi.org/10.1016/S0022-1031(03)00056-8.

5 Stephen B. Fawcett and L. Keith Miller, "Training Public-Speaking Behavior: An Experimental Analysis and Social Validation," *Journal of Applied Behavior Analysis* 8, no. 2 (1975): 125-35, dx.doi.org/10.1901%2Fjaba.1975.8-125.

6 John A. Daly, Anita L. Vangelisti, and Samuel G. Lawrence, "Self-Focused Attention and Public Speaking Anxiety," *Personality and Individual Differences* 10, no. 8 (1989): 903–13, doi.org/10.1016/0191-8869(89)90025-1.

7 Mel Slater, David-Paul Pertaub, and Anthony Steed, "Public Speaking in Virtual Reality: Facing an Audience of Avatars," *IEEE Computer Graphics and Applications* 19, no. 2 (1999), 6–9, doi.org/10.1109/38.749116.

8 Simon Sinek, "How to Leverage Being an Introvert," YouTube, November 25, 2020, youtu.be/ozSjz6iRKSA?t=80.

9 Bodie, "A Racing Heart, Rattling Knees, and Ruminative Thoughts."

10 Karl MacGinty, "Woods Reveals the Man behind the Mask," *Independent*, July 25, 2006, independent.ie/sport/golf/woods-reveals-the-real-man-behind-mask-26376101.html.

Conclusion: Moving Millions

1 Brené Brown, "Brené with Barack Obama on Leadership, Family & Service," *Dare to Lead* podcast, December 7, 2020, 42:35.

2 "*Hamilton* Surpasses $1 Billion in Revenue after Disney Sale," Ticketing Business News, June 9, 2020, theticketingbusiness.com/2020/06/09/hamilton-surpasses-1bn-revenue-disney-sale.

RESOURCES
NOTEWORTHY TALKS

Here's a list of the talks I've referenced in the book. For a soft copy of the list with clickable hyperlinks, visit podiumconsulting .com/talks. Some are so good you'll want to watch them more than once.

Achor, Shawn. "The Happy Secret to Better Work." Filmed May 2011. TED. ted.com/talks/shawn_achor_the_happy_secret_to_better_work.

Allende, Isabel. "Tales of Passion." Filmed March 2007. TED. ted.com/talks/ isabel_allende_tales_of_passion.

Ariely, Dan. "What Makes Us Feel Good about Our Work?" Filmed October 2012. TED. ted.com/talks/dan_ariely_what_makes_us_feel_good_ about_our_work.

Brown, Brené. "Listening to Shame." Filmed March 2012. TED. ted.com/ talks/brene_brown_listening_to_shame.

Brown, Brené. "The Power of Vulnerability." Filmed June 2010. TED. ted. com/talks/brene_brown_the_power_of_vulnerability.

Cain, Susan. "The Power of Introverts." Filmed February 2012. TED. ted. com/talks/susan_cain_the_power_of_introverts.

Cutts, Matt. "Try Something New for 30 Days." Filmed March 2011. TED. ted.com/talks/matt_cutts_try_something_new_for_30_days.

Fonda, Jane. "Life's Third Act." Filmed December 2011. TED. ted.com/talks/ jane_fonda_life_s_third_act.

Gawande, Atul. "How Do We Heal Medicine?" Filmed March 2012. TED. ted. com/talks/atul_gawande_how_do_we_heal_medicine.

Gladwell, Malcolm. "Choice, Happiness, and Spaghetti Sauce." Filmed February 2004. TED. ted.com/talks/malcolm_gladwell_choice_happiness_and_spaghetti_sauce.

Headlee, Celeste. "10 Ways to Have a Better Conversation." Filmed May 2015. TED. ted.com/talks/celeste_headlee_10_ways_to_have_a_better_conversation.

Lewinsky, Monica. "The Price of Shame." Filmed March 2015. TED. ted.com/talks/monica_lewinsky_the_price_of_shame.

Little, Brian. "Who Are You, Really? The Puzzle of Personality." Filmed February 2016. TED. ted.com/talks/brian_little_who_are_you_really_the_puzzle_of_personality.

Marsh, Nigel. "How to Make Work-Life Balance Work." Filmed May 2010. TED. ted.com/talks/nigel_marsh_how_to_make_work_life_balance_work.

Miller, B.J. "What Really Matters at the End of Life." Filmed March 2015. TED. ted.com/talks/bj_miller_what_really_matters_at_the_end_of_life.

Oliver, Jamie. "Teach Every Child about Food." Filmed February 2010. TED. ted.com/talks/jamie_oliver_teach_every_child_about_food.

Perel, Esther. "Rethinking Infidelity: A Talk for Anyone Who Has Ever Loved." Filmed March 2015. TED. ted.com/talks/esther_perel_rethinking_infidelity_a_talk_for_anyone_who_has_ever_loved.

Pink, Dan. "The Puzzle of Motivation." Filmed July 2009. TED. ted.com/talks/dan_pink_the_puzzle_of_motivation.

Puddicombe, Andy. "All It Takes Is 10 Mindful Minutes." Filmed November 2012. TED. ted.com/talks/andy_puddicombe_all_it_takes_is_10_mindful_minutes.

Robbins, Tony. "Why We Do What We Do." Filmed February 2006. TED. ted.com/talks/tony_robbins_why_we_do_what_we_do.

Robinson, Sir Ken. "Do Schools Kill Creativity?" Filmed February 2006. TED. ted.com/talks/sir_ken_robinson_do_schools_kill_creativity.

Sandberg, Sheryl. "Why We Have Too Few Women Leaders." Filmed December 2010. TED. ted.com/talks/sheryl_sandberg_why_we_have_too_few_women_leaders.

Sinek, Simon. "How Great Leaders Inspire Action." Filmed September 2009. TED. ted.com/talks/simon_sinek_how_great_leaders_inspire_action.

Stevenson, Bryan. "You Don't Create Justice by Doing What Is Comfortable." Filmed October 20, 2015. Google Zeitgeist. youtube.com/watch?v=0Ufwi36Fdq8.

Suzuki, Wendy. "The Brain-Changing Benefits of Exercise." Filmed November 2017. TED. ted.com/talks/wendy_suzuki_the_brain_changing_benefits_of_exercise.

Vanderkam, Laura. "How to Gain Control of Your Free Time." Filmed October 2016. TED. ted.com/talks/laura_vanderkam_how_to_gain_control_of_your_free_time.

Veitch, James. "This Is What Happens When You Reply to Spam Email." Filmed December 2015. TED. ted.com/talks/james_veitch_this_is_what_happens_when_you_reply_to_spam_email.

Velásquez, Lizzie. "How Do You Define Yourself?" Filmed December 2013. TED. ted.com/talks/lizzie_velasquez_how_do_you_define_yourself.

Wilson, Taylor. "Yup, I Built a Nuclear Fusion Reactor." Filmed March 2012. TED. ted.com/talks/taylor_wilson_yup_i_built_a_nuclear_fusion_reactor.

Zander, Benjamin. "The Transformative Power of Classical Music." Filmed February 2008. TED. ted.com/talks/benjamin_zander_the_transformative_power_of_classical_music.